DEVELOPING
COUNSELLOR SUPERVISION

Developing Counselling, edited by Windy Dryden, is an innovative series of books which provides counsellors and counselling trainees with practical hints and guidelines on the problems they face in the counselling process. The books assume that readers have a working knowledge of the approach in question, and, in a clear and accessible fashion show how the counsellor can more effectively translate that knowledge into everyday practice.

Books in the series include:

Developing the Practice of Counselling
Windy Dryden and Colin Feltham

Developing Counsellor Supervision
Colin Feltham and Windy Dryden

Developing Counsellor Training
Windy Dryden and Colin Feltham

Developing Person-Centred Counselling
Dave Mearns

Developing Psychodynamic Counselling
Brendan McLaughlin

DEVELOPING
COUNSELLOR SUPERVISION

Colin Feltham and Windy Dryden

SAGE Publications
London • Thousand Oaks • New Delhi

First published 1994
Reprinted 1995, 1998, 1999

SAGE Publications Ltd
6 Bonhill Street
London EC2A 4PU

SAGE Publications Inc
2455 Teller Road
Thousand Oaks, California 91320

SAGE Publications India Pvt Ltd
32, M-Block Market
Greater Kailash – I
New Delhi 110 048

British Library Cataloguing in Publication Data

Feltham, Colin
   Developing Counsellor Supervision. –
   (Developing Counselling Series)
   I. Title   II. Dryden, Windy   III. Series
   361.323

ISBN 0–8039–8938–5
ISBN 0–8039–8939–3 (pbk)

Library of Congress catalog card number 94–065542

Typeset by Mayhew Typesetting, Rhayader, Powys
Printed and bound in Great Britain by
Biddles Ltd, Guildford and King's Lynn

Contents

Introduction

Like its companion volumes, this book is addressed primarily to those practitioners who have some experience in the field. However, it should also be of interest to counsellor trainees who have a need to know what is involved in supervision and to counsellors who may be intending to train as supervisors. As well as being aimed at beginning supervisors, we hope that experienced supervisors may find certain features of the book useful. We assume that readers come from a variety of theoretical persuasions, work in a great many settings and are exposed to a variety of influences and demands. We have addressed the book mainly to those engaged in one-to-one supervision of individual counselling but pointers may be extrapolated for group and peer supervision and for the supervision of couple and group counselling.

Counsellor supervision has begun to receive close attention within the last few years. Although it has always been understood as an ethical and professional necessity for practising counsellors, supervision in Britain has not been researched, understood and presented on training courses as adequately as it might have been. Relatively little literature and training material has appeared here, although what has is stimulating (see for example, Mattinson, 1975; Inskipp and Proctor, 1989; Hawkins and Shohet, 1989). Since counsellor training in Britain still predominantly follows the historical influence of the psychoanalytic and person-centred traditions, what has been written and what is presented in supervision training often emulates these influences. We hope in this book to bring some balance from the eclectic, integrative and cognitive-behavioural orientations which have been steadily gaining ground in Britain.

Comprehensive American accounts of supervision theory and practice may be found in Hess (1980); Bradley (1989); and Bernard and Goodyear (1992). An excellent concise account of the history of and research into supervision is given by Holloway (1992). It is our intention to present here a variety of practical approaches to supervision culled from different models of counselling, which readers may consider and use eclectically, as befits their own situation. We have included certain material as Appendices which we ourselves have found helpful as supervisors, and we have made a significant number of references to the supervision literature.

It is important from the outset to give thought to the question of what supervision is and is not, and why it is viewed, for example by the British Association for Counselling, as a sine qua non of the practising counsellor's professional life. Unfortunately the term 'supervision' still carries connotations of managerial oversight and control, mistrust and coercion of the worker by an employer. This is, of course, a long way from its meaning in a counselling context, where it applies to a professional, consultative, supportive aid for counsellors. Although supervision does indeed have a rather sober ethical dimension, safeguarding clients from potential abuse by counsellors, it also aims to promote effective counselling by assisting counsellors in their professional development. From the training supervision of beginning counsellors through to the collegial consultation of experienced practitioners, supervision is dedicated to helping clients by helping their counsellors. Supervision is always, ultimately, focused on helping the client, even if this sometimes entails spending time examining counsellors' and supervisors' own feelings and interpersonal dynamics.

One of the first lessons for supervisors to learn is to distinguish between supervision and counselling. Every supervisor must have a first session in the role of supervisor, which may be somewhat unnerving. There is no way of avoiding such experiences or making them easier, even when trainee supervisees may have role-played supervision sessions before actually commencing work as a supervisor. In some ways, then, supervision recapitulates the first-hand learning of beginning counsellors. Supervision can, however, feel at first like counselling at one remove, attempting to help the counsellor to help an initially distant client. The first steps in supervision can feel awkward as you try to become quickly accustomed to your new role in relation to the supervisee and in relation to the (now distant) client. Because of this natural awkwardness, it is understandable that many beginning supervisors may unwittingly find themselves counselling their supervisees. Another understandable faltering first step is to emulate one's own supervisors. We mention these experiences to underscore the fact that no training course or book can substitute for learning from direct and sometimes 'painful' experience in the 'deep end'.

We hope that this small book will assist in the development of counsellor supervision in its diverse settings, thus improving the services offered to clients. We anticipate that interesting trends within the counselling world, for example the provision of counselling in employee assistance programmes and GPs' surgeries, will generate demands for greater effectiveness and accountability, and that this will in turn place greater demands on supervisors and trainers.

Colin Feltham
Windy Dryden

Acknowledgements

The authors would like to express their gratitude to the authors and publishers for permission to reprint the following:

Appendix 1 Presenting a client for supervision. Ian Horton (1993) 'Supervision', in R. Bayne and P. Nicolson (eds) *Counselling and Psychology for Health Professionals*. London: Chapman and Hall. Reprinted by permission of Chapman and Hall.

Appendix 2 BAC *Code of Ethics and Practice for the Supervision of Counsellors* (1988). Reprinted by permission of the British Association for Counselling.

Appendix 3 Therapist intentions. C. Hill and K.E. O'Grady (1985) 'List of therapist intentions illustrated in a case study and with therapists of varying theoretical orientations'. *Journal of Counseling Psychology*, 32: 3–22. © 1985 Reprinted by permission of the American Psychological Association.

Appendix 4 Competencies of supervisors. ACES Supervision Interest Network; AACD Convention (2 April 1985).

Appendix 5 BAC Recognition of Supervisors details (1993). Reprinted by permission of the British Association for Counselling.

Every effort has been made to trace all the copyright holders, but if any have been inadvertently overlooked the publishers will be pleased to make the necessary arrangements at the first opportunity.

Creating a
Supervisory Alliance

1 Exchange views with supervisees on supervision and initiate a mutually acceptable contract

Counsellors who approach you for supervision on a paying basis are likely to be much more knowledgeable about what is involved in negotiations relating to counselling than a client approaching a counsellor. However, some counsellors know little about supervision before receiving it. Some have been told that they must have it and do not quite understand why. This may seem surprising – and we certainly believe that any worthwhile counselling training should include explanation about the meaning, function and necessity of supervision – but such ignorance is still far from uncommon. This is, perhaps, the most fundamental reason for discovering what new supervisees understand by the term 'supervision'.

If you supervise within a training course, perhaps in a small group of trainees who have completed some initial training, your supervisees may not ask you what supervision consists of or consider that they have any right to question you, because they may have no choice of who is supervising them: you may have been presented as a 'course requirement'. In this situation, where supervisees apparently have little choice or room for negotiation, it is still necessary to discover what they mean by supervision and what they think they may need. Whatever restrictions you and your supervisees may be working under, there is always some room (if not a necessity, according to Bordin, 1983) for discussion and negotiation. Furthermore, it is poor practice to make assumptions, to proceed without clarification and to erode supervisees' own power.

If you supervise within an organization, voluntary or statutory, you may be the only supervisory resource available to counsellors in that setting. In that case, they again may have no apparent choice. They will have to accept you as their supervisor, along with your style of supervision, your theoretical orientation and any organizational bias you may have. But here again, there is still room for explanation, discussion and negotiation. We are perhaps assuming here that all counsellor supervisors understand the need for adult, egalitarian discussion and contract-making. Whatever your organizational or assessment role may be in relation to supervisees, you cannot form a productive supervisory relationship with them on the basis of a purely authoritarian attitude. (See Section 4, however, on what attitudes supervisees may prefer at different stages of development, and consult Fisher (1989).)

We suggest that one of the very first questions you ask is 'What do you know about supervision?' You can expand on this by asking whether the person has received previous supervision, has read anything about it, has been taught anything about it or has any fantasy or anticipation of what it may involve. These questions are, of course, suitable for beginning counsellors. The less knowledge about or experience of supervision the person has, the more time you will probably need to spend exploring these fundamental issues. Do not accept facile assurances that your new supervisee understands what supervision is if you suspect that he or she is wary of admitting any ignorance or uncertainty. You may well spend an entire first session or two simply discussing the meaning and uses of supervision. It can be helpful to suggest to the supervisee that they listen to Inskipp and Proctor's (1989) audiotape *Being Supervised*, which explores these very issues. Horton (1993) provides a very useful guide for supervisees on how to present cases in supervision, which is reproduced in Appendix 1.

Depending on whether you as a supervisor have considerable or minimal supervisory experience, you may have forgotten, or still be in touch with, the high levels of anxiety that beginning counsellors often carry into their supervision. Skovholt and Ronnestad (1992a) refer to this as a 'pervasive anxiety' and argue that beginning supervisees often attempt to disguise this anxiety by appearing more confident than they really are. They may well attribute great authority to you and fail to ask the kinds of questions to which they need answers. Anticipate this by describing your outlook on supervision, your experience, theoretical orientation and any preferences for supervisory foci. Help the supervisee to question you on these and other issues. Raise the question of fees, cancellation policy, frequency of sessions, confidentiality and other boundaries. While it is not helpful to bombard supervisees with these issues, they do need to be discussed in a first session. Some issues may not become apparent until work begins (for example, conflict about the use of tape-recordings, or areas in which the supervisor has no expertise) and will need to be handled clearly and honestly when they do arise.

The pervasive anxiety of the beginning supervisee may also be addressed by clarifying the extent of your assessment role, if any, as well as any organizational or even statutory responsibility you may have. The concept of 'negligent supervision' has no real teeth as yet in Britain but in the USA counsellor supervisors may be considered 'vicariously liable' in law suits for their supervisees' errors (Austin et al., 1990). If you believe, as a supervisor, that you carry particular responsibilities for your supervisees, these must be made absolutely clear to them at the outset. Vagueness may feed supervisees' anxiety (see Sections 2 and 28 for further discussion of these issues).

Let supervisees know as much about your work as they need to know and, equally, ask for the kind of information you require before committing yourself to a supervision contract. You need this information not only from individual counsellors but also from any course directors or trainers who ask you to supervise on their training courses. You must satisfy yourself that any courses or individual supervisees you are associated with meet your own standards of practice and ethics. You may want to know what previous clinical experience your new supervisee has, what level of training has been reached, what supportive networks he or she has besides you and what kinds of client groups the supervisee is working with. All these matters should be aired in a first session or sessions. Because it is not always possible to gather this information meaningfully out of context, you may invite the supervisee in a first session to describe a current case briefly, in order to afford both of you an opportunity to sample each other's needs, abilities and ways of working.

It is not too unusual to be asked urgently for supervision by counsellors who have suddenly run into difficulties and/or who have not had recent supervision. In such a case, while you may agree to take a supervisee on, do not allow his or her urgency to sweep aside the need for contractual clarity. In this and all other first meetings with supervisees, spend some time mutually examining a definition and understanding of supervision. When you have substantially covered the kinds of issues raised here, go on to formulate a working agreement. Proctor (1987) suggests that a cooperative agreement be reached, based on an understanding of accountability for counsellor effectiveness, counsellor self-responsibility, supervisor responsibility and the willingness of both supervisor and counsellor to develop and maintain their respective skills.

The formality with which such agreements are made may vary considerably, but should ideally always include statements by the

supervisor and supervisee on their separate and joint responsibilities and needs. The supervisor may agree to provide or facilitate
safety, to offer stimulation, challenge and professional knowledge;
the supervisee may agree to present significant clinical issues, to
ask for specific feedback and to be open to challenge. These
agreements may be reviewed from time to time and amended in
the light of experience. Contracts made between very experienced
supervisors and supervisees may contain different issues but should
also be clear and professional.

Key point

Raise and discuss fully issues relating to your own and your
supervisees' experience, current work and supervisory
requirements and arrive at a mutually agreeable contract
before commencing a supervisory relationship.

---

2   Discuss and explore the issues
involved in the BAC *Code of
Ethics and Practice for the
Supervision of Counsellors*

Counsellor supervisors do not necessarily come from a counselling
background (many are psychotherapists or clinical psychologists,
for example) and are not necessarily BAC members. All counsellor
supervisors should subscribe to a professional code of ethics,
however, and most of these will agree on the fundamentals of good
practice. We argue here that you should formally address with your
supervisees, in whatever context you see them, the issues
contained in the BAC *Code of Ethics and Practice for the
Supervision of Counsellors* (see Appendix 2). You cannot assume
that supervisees are familiar with the Code and if you and they
believe that it simply replicates the *Code of Ethics and Practice for
Counsellors*, you need to examine it because in fact it is not a
simple replication. Sometimes informal, unspoken assumptions
about supervision predominate, for example that it is simply an

empty formality, that it is utterly different from counselling, far less intense than counselling, far more intellectual and collegial than counselling, and so on. Examination of the Code together with your supervisees is one important way of checking on what assumptions each of you has.

We look at the distinctions between supervision, training and personal therapy in Section 3 and at other boundary issues in Section 6. Here we will take a few examples of ethical and professional questions for supervisors to consider. Confidentiality, for example, is often assumed to be in effect without really considering its parameters. As in counselling itself, it is good practice in supervision to discuss exactly what these parameters may be. The supervisory relationship is likely to be confidential between the individual supervisor and counsellor (except where the supervision takes place in a group, of course, when wider boundaries necessarily apply) but to have certain caveats. What are these?:

1 The supervisor has a need to take material from his or her supervision of counsellors to his or her own supervisor, consultant or manager.
2 The supervisor has a responsibility to monitor the competency and ethical practice of supervisees and has the right in certain cases to alert third parties to concerns about supervisees (for example, any serious suspicion that a supervisee is a danger to him- or herself or to others).
3 The supervisor may be engaged in research, writing or applying for his or her own BAC recognition as a supervisor, in which case the supervisor may seek the supervisee's permission to record sessions and to present material to others.
4 The supervisor may be working within a training course and may be required formally to report to a course director or other tutors on the progress of his or her supervisees.

The first two of these are built into the ethical requirements of counsellors and supervisors. Even so, it may be helpful to clarify with supervisees whether you intend to refer to them by name in your own supervision and whether you guarantee to preserve the anonymity of their clients. It is helpful to clarify exactly what constitutes any 'danger to him- or herself or to others'. Consider, on the one hand, how anxiety-inducing this may sound to a new supervisee already suffering from 'pervasive anxiety', and on the other how familiar and reassuring it may sound. Concern for integrity and competency should permeate the counselling profession. The obvious examples of 'danger' are indications that a counsellor is seriously abusing clients sexually, financially or emotionally, or where he or she is seriously negligent. The counsellor may become dangerous either through incompetency or through his or her own compromised mental health. As in counselling, it is wise first to broach such concerns directly with the supervisee and to ask him or her to take suitable actions (for example, by entering personal therapy, terminating with a particular client or withdrawing from counselling altogether). If the supervisee refuses, you have the right, indeed responsibility, to take steps independently. These steps might include your speaking with your supervisee's colleagues or line manager, if any, and reporting him or her to the BAC or any other organization with which the supervisee is affiliated.

The third point, relating to research, writing and supervisor recognition, is open to negotiation, but certainly permission to use any material from supervision should always be sought and agreed. The fourth point, however, is perhaps more contentious. If you supervise trainees in a group, for example, and your agreement with a course director is that you will formally engage in assessment of your supervisees and will verbally report on them to the director, then this is an explicit arrangement that should be clearly relayed to supervisees. They may not like it but they have presumably bought into a training which specifies that this is a requirement. On some courses, it is explicitly stated that supervision will in fact be confidential and that supervisors will not participate in assessment. On some courses, however, the situation may not be so clear. Supervisors may be asked for informal feedback on supervisees' progress, or they may suddenly encounter urgent difficulties or dilemmas in relation to particular supervisees which they wish to discuss with other tutors. It may not be possible to account for every eventuality in advance, but the guiding principle should be clarity, honesty and agreement from the outset.

It is worth considering whether confidentiality should also apply in reverse. For example, if you as the supervisor disclose certain information about yourself or about some of your own previous clients, in the interests of helping the supervisee, is it agreed that the supervisee will keep this information confidential? Are there any unspoken grey areas connected with confidentiality? For example, are we permitted to discuss material from supervision within our own personal therapy? If we agree that we may speak with consultants, exactly who are these consultants? A judgement may have to be made between what is too obsessional and what is too vague.

Section 28 considers possible forms of obvious and subtle abuse within counselling. There has been much recent discussion about the prevalence and unacceptability of sexual contact between counsellors and their clients (Rutter, 1990; Russell, 1993) but little similar discussion about sex between supervisors and supervisees. The Code states that there should be 'clear boundaries between working relationships and friendships or other relationships' and that supervisors 'should not exploit this [the supervisory] relationship'. This is generally taken to mean that however collegial supervision may be, it should remain a working relationship which models the boundaries expected in counselling and should on no account become a sexual relationship. There is anecdotal evidence that this taboo is taken far less seriously than that relating to counsellors and clients. Full discussion of the Code and its ramifications is likely to produce a clarity and framework in which these and other issues do not begin to erode the effectiveness of supervision. One practical way of facilitating such discussion is to ask a new supervisee to read the Code before a second session and to bring back any queries he or she may have.

Key point

Study and introduce supervisees to the BAC *Code of Ethics and Practice for the Supervision of Counsellors*, and discuss as fully as possible your understanding of what impact this has on the agreement you make together.

---

3   Discuss and clarify the boundaries between supervision, personal therapy and training

The BAC *Code of Ethics and Practice for the Supervision of Counsellors* specifically states that supervision is 'not primarily concerned with' training or with the personal counselling of the counsellor. The supervisor's central task is to oversee the work between counsellor and client and the supervisor should therefore not become, unintentionally or intentionally, the supervisee's trainer or counsellor. As the Code recognizes, there are often inevitable elements of training and even personal therapy within supervision. There is some debate about these boundaries, which are not universally accepted. For example, the psychoanalytic tradition of the 'training analysis' fuses, to some extent, the training and personal therapy elements in therapists' professional development. In the person-centred tradition, the emphasis on the genuine client–counsellor relationship is mirrored in the genuineness of the supervisee–supervisor relationship. In rational emotive behaviour therapy, supervision may often contain instructional elements which are intimately linked with both training and personal therapy (Wessler and Ellis, 1980). Our own view, broadly speaking, is that you should not allow supervision to become the counselling of the supervisee, but you would do well to note and focus on instances when supervisees may indeed benefit from supervisory interventions that address them as people who are sometimes in distress or confusion.

Critics of the professionalization of counselling sometimes argue that the increasing divisions between counselling, supervision, training (and indeed counselling skills, advice-giving, befriending and psychotherapy) do not serve the interests of clients but those of the professional elite who seek to exclude outsiders and to generate 'jobs for the boys' (Howard, 1992). Such criticisms should not be dismissed out of hand and we suggest that supervisors and trainers consider their roles carefully rather than uncritically accepting current practice. Our purpose here, however, is to address the positive aspects of the differentiation between supervision, personal therapy and training.

Supervision and personal therapy

It is undoubtedly the case that counsellors sometimes, if not often, run into difficulties or impasses, or experience recurrent problems or blind spots with clients, because there is a residual, unexamined or unresolved problem or conflict in their own lives or personalities. There may be characterological problems which may require long-term and in-depth personal work to modify or transform them; there may be particular 'single-issue' problematic traits that could benefit from quite specific interventions; or there may be pressing current life events which produce stress that interferes with counsellors' occupational effectiveness. Such problems may emerge within supervision in obvious instances of direct countertransference or they may only become apparent as a subtle behaviour pattern to the supervisor over the course of time. The core issue is that you must consider to what extent you deal with the personal material of the supervisee. We will look closely at some examples (which are anonymous amalgams of actual supervisees) and raise questions in each case which may provoke reflection.

Nigel is a recently qualified counsellor who appears to agonize over most of his clients. To the supervisor he seems to be a highly anxious, perfectionistic person who believes that he should be doing better with his clients and that they should be making faster progress. The supervisor judges that Nigel is probably performing better than he gives himself credit for and that most of his clients appear to be gaining some benefit from his counselling. However, it seems likely that Nigel will experience considerable stress unless he addresses his own anxiety and that he will probably convey some of this anxiety to his clients. Should the supervisor encourage Nigel to re-enter therapy (and a particular kind of therapy), should he *insist* that Nigel re-enters therapy, should he help Nigel to examine his anxiety in detail in relation to certain clients, or should he help Nigel to see that he might work better with some clients rather than others?

Sarah is an experienced counsellor whose competency is not doubted by her supervisor. Increasingly in supervision sessions, however, she begins to talk about instances from her own life. She has recently separated from her partner and is having financial difficulties. This does not seem to be affecting her work but it is clear that she is indirectly asking for your help with her own problems. You are sympathetic towards her plight and you realize that she cannot afford to pay for further personal therapy at this time in her life. Will you tacitly allow her to continue to discuss her problems within supervision, will you explicitly tell her that you are prepared to devote some supervision time to these concerns, will you insist that she should get some therapy and that she can afford it if she really wants to, or will you insist that you are not prepared to spend any further time listening to these problems in supervision?

These two examples illustrate some of the dilemmas facing supervisors in relation to supervisees who may need personal therapy. Our own guiding policy in such cases is that we are prepared to intervene directly if a very small amount of pragmatic and humane counselling will help. When this becomes protracted and overshadows client concerns, or threatens to do so, or when it detracts from the task of supervision in any way, then this indicates a need for strongly recommending that the supervisee secures personal therapy. You may also encounter the supervisee who is actually in therapy but still has obvious personal limitations: would you consider suggesting that the supervisee changes his or her therapist? Some counsellors model themselves on their own counsellors or therapists in such a way that they fail to develop their own style or to offer interventions from which clients might benefit more. The crux of the supervision–counselling interface is this: as the supervisor you must make decisions about how much and what kind of help you offer (or deny) the supervisee, bearing in mind that it is the *client's* interests that are really paramount. It can be tempting to slip into counsellor mode when you might identify something in your supervisee that you could well address with your counselling skills, but how will this affect the future of your supervisory relationship? Discuss this concern with the supervisee.

Supervision and training

A very close relationship often exists on training courses between training supervision (whether individually or in groups) and other course components. Trainees who are beginning to work with clients are at that point in their development where they are putting theory and skills into practice and need help with this task. This sort of help is necessarily often tutorial and instructional in nature. Brammer and Wassmer (1977) refer to 'combination didactic-experiential supervision' which is exactly this kind of benign overlap. It is impossible to separate training from purely supervisory elements in the supervision process, since supervisees are likely to gain implicit training from their supervisors' interventions. It may also be undesirable to withhold certain explicit instances of micro-training within supervision, when these would be ethically justified as furthering the interests of the client under discussion. Again, one or two examples will illustrate the dilemmas.

Gillian is working with a client who, it turns out, has some unresolved problems stemming from an earlier trauma of being involved in a violent incident. The client is becoming very agitated and is experiencing flashbacks. The supervisor happens to have had a great deal of experience working with post-traumatic stress and has some very clear ideas about what would help this client. Should the supervisor withhold this knowledge, encourage Gillian simply to 'stay with the client's process', drop a few hints or suggest some appropriate literature, self-disclose or offer explicitly to train Gillian briefly in one or two effective techniques dealing with PTSD?

Leroy is playing a tape-recording of a recent session with a client, and he expresses concern about some of his interventions. He says that he wanted to get across his concern to the client but could not quite find an acceptable way to do this. He asks you to help him. Do you simply prompt Leroy to think of alternative responses, do you try to get him to examine why he may be blocking himself, do you carefully go over the interventions in question and encourage brainstorming, or do you make certain suggestions in the form of a brief micro-skills training intervention?

Again, these examples show that careful judgement is required, not to say common sense, when deciding how to interpret the taboo on merging supervision with training or personal therapy. The clearest sign of unhelpfully straying from one to the other is when supervisees persistently seek either personal therapy or training from their supervisor and when their clients all but disappear from the supervisory focus. In these cases, you certainly need to suggest to supervisees that they investigate sources of alternative help or training. But do this sensitively and encourage debate on your reasoning. We are quite prepared to offer a certain degree of micro-training in such cases, provided that it is kept in proportion and does not displace core supervisory tasks.

You also need to consider your position if, as a trainer or supervisor, you are approached by a student or supervisee who asks you for personal counselling. It is considered by the BAC and by many practitioners that it is best to keep clear boundaries and therefore not to accept such invitations. Sometimes there may be an overlap, for example when you have been counselling someone who subsequently begins training on a course with which you are involved. It is necessary to discuss such instances explicitly in order to avoid any misunderstandings or embarrassment. Some training institutes seem to foster a rather incestuous climate in which students are receiving counselling from their trainers and supervisors, or from close colleagues of their trainers and supervisors. We think this should be avoided wherever possible.

Key point

Consult professional guidelines on the boundaries between supervision, training and personal therapy, along with your own and your supervisees' interpretations of these, and monitor and act on any compromising of these boundaries with due consideration.

---

4 Offer supervision that is congruent with supervisees' stages of development

Clearly, there is a very wide range of abilities between beginning counsellors and highly experienced counsellors. Various schemata have been put forward to describe the stages involved (Stoltenberg and Delworth, 1987; Hawkins and Shohet, 1989; Ronnestad and Skovholt, 1993). Common sense tells us that there are likely to be significant developmental differences between the counsellor-in-training and the counsellor of 40 years' experience, for example. 'Developmental supervision' can also refer to a particularly psychodynamic view, which suggests that supervisees may follow a logical progression of dependency, idealization, disappointment and autonomy in relation to their supervisors, in much the same way that some clients work through a relationship with their counsellors. Bradley (1989) discusses supervisee development in terms of pre-conformist, conformist and post-conformist levels, which refer roughly to the stages of indiscipline, orthodoxy and mature practice. Yet other commentators suggest that the field of supervision is so complex that a developmental view may sometimes be limited or unhelpful (Worthington, 1987). Here we take the view that supervisors would do well to consider how developmental factors may affect their work. Hawkins and Shohet (1989) believe counsellors may be described in the following terms.

The novice: This is the trainee, who is naturally characterized by lack of experience and attendant anxiety, but also by optimism and enthusiasm. Novices are struggling to put theory into practice and to perform well in order to meet assessment criteria. They may view their first cases in rather concrete terms. They usually lack experience of different clients and of different client groups and are therefore hampered by not being able to compare experiences of clients. Novices may need more structured and didactic supervision.

The apprentice: While the trainee is highly dependent on the trainer and supervisor, the apprentice is moving towards greater autonomy. The apprentice becomes more discriminating as he or she realizes that clients differ and that different strategies are suitable on different occasions. Apprentices may become somewhat disillusioned after the honeymoon period of training has ended. Counsellors in this stage of development may wonder whether they will become effective counsellors and their supervision may need to be oriented towards 'emotional holding'.

The journeyperson: At this stage the counsellor is experiencing his or her own competency and is considerably less dependent on the supervisor. The counsellor can adapt to individual clients and can hold an overview of the counselling relationship, the client's intrapsychic dynamics and their external circumstances and social context. By this stage the counsellor will have internalized the theoretical approach in which he or she was trained. Supervision is likely to include more challenge, mutual disclosure and a generally collegial climate.

The master craftsperson: At this stage the counsellor will have integrated a great deal of learning and clinical experience and will probably be working as a supervisor or trainer him- or herself. The 'master practitioner' may have transcended his or her particular training orientation to become a self-motivated researcher. This counsellor's practice will be stable and the counsellor will be aware of his or her own strengths and shortcomings, as well as the limitations of the counselling field generally. According to Goldberg the master practitioner is 'one who has brought his/her training, sensitivity, perceptiveness, compassion, intelligence and motivation to the clinical work and has shaped these resources and skills so that they are no longer "techniques", but rather an integral part of the therapist' (1992: 76). The purpose of supervision in this stage may be to monitor the counsellor so that he or she does not become immune to criticism or innovation and to offer external, and sometimes specialized, perspectives.

This is a possible map of discernible stages. Other writers are satisfied with a distinction between beginning and advanced practitioners. Still others put forward even more elaborate developmental maps (see for example, Skovholt and Ronnestad, 1992b).

Many factors complicate the kind of map given above, including individual differences between even beginning counsellors, the effects of different theoretical orientations (and the extent to which these are shared by counsellors and supervisors), the quality and level of training received by the supervisee, the relative clinical and supervisory experience of the supervisor and the contexts in which supervision takes place. Against the background of this complexity we proceed cautiously to suggest certain lines of perspective and practice.

According to Reising and Daniels (1983) beginning counsellors tend to be anxious, dependent, technique-oriented and unready for confrontation. Other researchers point out that beginners seem to prefer a teaching style of supervision, with an emphasis on the learning and refining of skills and techniques within an emotionally supportive relationship. The finding of Fisher (1989) that beginning supervisees preferred an 'authoritarian' style over an egalitarian one, suggests that an optimal supervisory style with beginners may be of a warmly authoritative kind. How supervisors respond to beginning counsellors' anxiety and dependency will also vary according to orientation. While person-centred supervisors will presumably offer a somewhat nurturant supervisory relationship in the beginning, rational emotive behavioural supervisors (Dryden, 1991a) tend to challenge supervisees' irrational thinking from the outset, in keeping with the principles of rational emotive behaviour therapy (REBT). Reports on the experiences of beginning super- visees (Cohen, 1980; Moore, 1991) confirm high levels of anxiety about assessment of performance and about the choice of counselling as a career. Bradley (1989) identifies several kinds of beginning anxiety, including performance and approval anxiety and dominance anxiety (the latter signifying that the supervisee is hierarchically 'one down' from the supervisor and susceptible to unfair evaluation or abuse of power). It is important for supervisors to take these factors into consideration, especially when they do in fact have an assessment role (see Section 6).

As you recognize and supervise the apprentice and the journey- person, you will notice greater confidence on the part of supervisees both in their use of skills and their professional self- image. Skills become more integrated, conceptualization becomes clearer as the counsellor gains wider experience of different clients and is more likely to know what to ask for from supervision. Loganbill et al. (1982) utilize a three-stage model of supervision which aims to identify supervisees' functioning at any level of development in terms of stagnation, confusion and integration. Thus, 'naive unawareness' may characterize the stagnant novice, while the stagnant apprentice or journeyperson may be seen as simply being stuck with certain clients. Supervisee confusion indicates uncertain growth which can be facilitated by the supervisor until the point at which the supervisee achieves some degree of integration. Each of these three stages can be measured in terms of supervisees' skills, emotional awareness, issues of autonomy, identity, respect for individual differences, purpose and direction, personal motivation and professional ethics. The supervisor may decide to employ facilitative, confrontative, catalytic or prescriptive interventions as fitting the particular kind of stagnation or confusion exhibited by the supervisee.

We have not dwelt here on supervisor development (see Section 30), but it is important to note the significance of matching (or otherwise) between supervisor and supervisee. It is often thought that beginning supervisees need very experienced supervisors who will be able to offer authority and emotional containment. Very inexperienced supervisors may have difficulty fulfilling this kind of role or, for example, may not be able to challenge supervisees when necessary. A counterargument to this is that experienced supervisors may often be distant in their own practice from the kinds of issues being faced by beginners, who may be helped better by colleagues only slightly senior to themselves. Hess (1986) points to the early anxieties which supervisors often have, based on their change of status and uncertain competencies. Supervisors in this position face the same dilemma as trainee counsellors who are expected to be both competent and honest, declaring their status openly to clients. It is unlikely that you can conceal your lack of supervisory experience and it is usually better (and certainly more ethical) to declare yourself honestly. At the same time, monitor the effect that your own stage of development may be having on that of your supervisee.

Key point

Acknowledge that supervisees may be at very different developmental stages, adjust your style and interventions accordingly and also allow for the many other influential variables in the supervisory relationship.

5   Offer supervision that is reasonably congruent with supervisees' own theoretical orientations

Trainee counsellors in Britain are increasingly likely to be learning a core theoretical model. This is largely because the Course Recognition Group of the British Association for Counselling stipulates that all courses applying for course recognition should be based on a clearly defined, coherent core model. This may mean a psychodynamic, person-centred, cognitive-behavioural or other specific theoretical orientation, or it may refer more broadly to a humanistic, transpersonal, psychoanalytic or behavioural approach (Dryden and Feltham, 1994a). Training courses are increasingly expected by the BAC to offer a core model which permeates all course elements and therefore a high proportion of trainees will expect to receive supervision that is congruent with the core model. This presents no difficulty in cases where supervisors are also course tutors or are specifically engaged because they are known to share the theoretical orientation of the course. There are instances, however, where difficulties may arise.

First, it is not unknown for course directors or other trainers to ask close colleagues to supervise students because they like and respect these colleagues, prefer to work with people they know and are confident that they have the right skills and experience. Sometimes such appointments are made without due regard for the question of whether supervisors share the theoretical orientation of the course. Appointing supervisors on this basis may often prove to be effective or at least not to be problematic, but it can go wrong. The belief that 'supervision is supervision' (that is, that all supervision is quite similar, regardless of orientation) is a dangerous one. We know of a supervisor from a person-centred background who found himself trying to supervise trainees who were being exposed to transactional analysis (TA) and who found his style 'woolly' in comparison with the apparently clear guidelines they were learning for TA diagnosis and treatment planning.

Second, because there is not always an abundance of work available for counsellors, supervisors and trainers, and much of the work is sessional and part-time, compromises are sometimes made. Candidates for such sessional work may be inclined (well-meaningly) to exaggerate how well versed they are in psychodynamic theory, for example, when in fact they have long ago grown bored with it and moved on to neurolinguistic programming (NLP). They may begin to supervise as psychodynamically as possible but progressively find themselves offering snippets of NLP. Our emotional attachment to certain theories and their practice is sometimes so strong that we cannot prevent ourselves from proselytizing.

Third, ostensibly eclectic or integrative courses, which are gaining in number, are sometimes quite unclear as to their theoretical underpinning. Some rely on trainees' intuitive, discretionary marrying of bits of theory from here and there, but this practice easily deteriorates into meaningless 'mishmash' eclecticism. If you are a highly experienced counsellor, you may be able to offer supervision which fits in well with an eclectic or integrative training. However, in our view there is considerable scope for misunderstanding here, especially when so-called eclecticism or integrationism is poorly defined and when supervisees and supervisors have their own interpretation of what they mean.

All the above problems are overcome at a stroke in those training programmes based on a single theoretical model and supported by a committed team of trainers and supervisors from the same 'stable'. Note, however, that some critics argue that this kind of homogeneity can become stultifying and that a pluralistic approach, in which conflict and debate are encouraged from the beginning, is far healthier (Samuels, 1989). According to this argument, there is no guarantee of competency in training and supervising everyone according to orthodox principles. This is an attractive argument but runs the risk, in practical terms, of dissolving into an unfocused eclecticism. There is good reason to suppose that beginners in fact need clearer theoretical structures than more advanced practitioners (see Section 4). One way in which a pluralistic outlook is certainly helpful, however, is that it can act as safeguard against the blindspots inherent in some purist models of counselling. In other words, a supervisor who is prepared to challenge the orthodoxy of the model, particularly in cases where the client might be better served by an alternative approach, is likely to offer greater protection to clients generally than supervisors who are uncritical towards the core model. In general, we suggest that a pluralistic outlook, and the kind of supervisory feedback associated with it, may be more helpful to the 'journeyperson' and 'master craftsperson' than to counsellors who are still consolidating their understanding (see Section 4).

In the case of certain pure theoretical models, it may be highly problematic for supervisors from alternative theoretical persuasions to offer adequate supervision. The explanations for psychological dysfunction and the purposeful therapeutic interventions belonging to rational emotive behaviour therapy and psychodynamic counselling, for example, are quite distinct and in many instances in obvious conflict. Trainees who are learning to apply psychodynamic theory in their early work with clients would be utterly confused by supervisory interventions originating from rational-emotive theory. To take an example:

Supervisee: Well, my client is constantly looking at the floor as if to avoid me, to resist my every glance . . . and also there are many long silences.
Supervisor: Have you agreed on a target problem?
Supervisee: Well, no, apart from initially discussing the presenting problem, no. The client has quite quickly regressed into . . .
Supervisor: How can you do productive work together without agreeing on a goal to work towards?
Supervisee: Sorry?

This brief dialogue is, of course, a caricature and we are not implying that either psychodynamic supervisees or rational emotive behavioural supervisors are this simplistic in practice. But the example begins to show that each of the parties involved has something completely different in mind: a different rationale, a different therapeutic procedure, a different language! It is unlikely that such an obvious mismatch would really occur, but variations on this theme of poor supervisor–supervisee alliance are probably common enough. Even within certain traditions, for example the Freudian and object-relations approaches within psychodynamic counselling, there are possibilities for misalliance. These factors do not necessarily prohibit offering supervision from an alternative perspective, but they do demand clarity and realism at the contracting stage if negative results are to be avoided.

According to Goodyear and Robyak (1982) 60 per cent of supervisors in the USA claimed to practise eclectically. There is no comparable study in the UK, but our impression is that there is a similar trend here. Counsellors who trained in one approach 10, 20 or 30 years ago are likely to have trained in or studied other approaches which have come to prominence only in recent years. It is also well documented (Goldberg, 1992) that seasoned counsellors and supervisors usually embrace a much broader view of human functioning and therapy than that in which they trained. Very experienced supervisors supervising experienced supervisees may very well achieve productive levels of rapport and enhanced practice, but again there is scope for mismatching. The seasoned counsellor supervising the inexperienced supervisee may in some cases be too distant from the supervisee's experience of anxiety, as well as the supervisee's exposure to current theory. For maximum effectiveness in the case of complex theories (such as transactional analysis) the supervisor should probably be simultaneously a trainer and researcher in that field.

Key point

Consider the advantages and in some cases necessity of having an agreed, clear, shared theoretical approach with supervisees and weigh this up against factors of eclecticism and relative experience.

---

6   Clarify any organizational, assessment, ethical and other responsibilities and boundaries

We have alluded to some of the areas which hold potential for misunderstanding and which may inadvertently sabotage supervision. Here we wish to extend this concern to the settings in which supervision takes place. This book is primarily addressed to counsellors but as Hawkins and Shohet (1989) and Inskipp and Proctor (1989) show, supervisors are often called to work with allied professionals (such as social workers, nurses, health visitors, residential workers) who may or may not have had extensive counsellor training. Managers of voluntary or commercial organizations sometimes request supervisors to work sessionally with their staff group and in such instances it is essential that boundaries are understood. Sometimes the manager *is* the supervisor, and may or may not have had training in counselling or counsellor supervision. Managers in this position should understand at the very least that their employee-supervisees may not feel able to disclose personal material to them, and hence the supervision may be less effective than that offered by an external supervisor. Each organization has its idiosyncratic traditions and expectations of staff, all of which affect the way the client is treated and therefore affect the responsibilities of the supervisor.

Imagine that you are a supervisor who is asked to supervise, on a fortnightly basis, a group of counsellors within a voluntary organization. The manager is enthusiastic for you to begin, the pay is generous and you need the money. On your first meeting with the staff group, however, you begin to realize that all is not well within the organization. The manager has assumed that he will participate in the supervision group. One of the staff tells you, in an aside, that the counsellors are unhappy with management and have little respect for their own line manager. You begin to realize that you have been invited into the proverbial hornet's nest. Now, we know from our own experience that this is not such an unusual scenario. We know too, as you probably do, what is supposed to happen in such a situation. According to the books (including this one!) you will assertively ask for a full and frank discussion of all issues, encouraging everyone to speak honestly, before attempting to agree on a contract for work. In reality, perhaps no one is prepared to be fully honest (the staff fear for their jobs) yet everyone wants this supervisory format to go ahead. You know you may be colluding with muted organizational conflicts if you go ahead on this basis, but you desperately need the money. What will you do?

The BAC *Code of Ethics and Practice for the Supervision of Counsellors* (Appendix 2) states that 'Supervisors who become aware of a conflict between their obligation to a counsellor and their obligation to an employing organization will make explicit to the counsellor the nature of the loyalties and responsibilities involved.' In the above scenario, if you follow our suggestion (Section 2) to have everyone concerned read and agree to the Code, then in this example you would have a clear reference point for addressing your dilemma. But you may not be immediately aware of a conflict of this kind or you may be uncertain how to interpret it. If a manager employs you and you agree a contract, is your obligation to the manager, the organization, its clients, its counsellors, or to whom? It is possible that your obligation may be more to the manager, and especially so if you are in fact employed within an organization. You may work in a multidisciplinary team in which your colleagues subscribe to a Code of Ethics that is somewhat at variance with your own; again, how will you settle such a difference? You owe some allegiance to your own professional body (whether BAC or another), to your employer, colleagues and clients, but common sense dictates that you are also responsible for your own livelihood and some compromise is often inevitable. Our view here is that unless your livelihood is indeed threatened, you should think very seriously before proceeding with any work that will compromise your professional effectiveness and integrity.

Suppose that you are asked by your line manager to assess and write a report on counsellors within the organization and that your report will form part of their performance appraisal. Will you agree, decline, compromise or be evasive? Or suppose that as a supervisor in private practice, you supervise a trainee who needs you to submit a written report after a year. Is there anything problematic in this? It is good practice in all such cases to be explicit with supervisees, to share any doubts or professional reservations you may have, and to encourage supervisees to air any misgivings they may have, before entering into or proceeding with a contract. In all cases where more parties are involved than the traditional triad of client, counsellor and supervisor, you must consider what ethical issues impinge on you. If, as a supervisor, you agree to write reports on a counsellor's work, clarify the following:

1 Who will read the report and how will it be kept confidential to those requiring to read it?
2 What will be the immediate and later effects of this report and at what stage, and by whom, will it be destroyed?
3 Does the report name or in any way identify clients or other people and if so have these people given consent?

Provided that you are satisfied on such points and that clients, supervisees and you are safeguarded by any necessary informed consent, then we believe that clear agreements on report writing should protect you from any later problems. Assessment procedures within training courses are likely to have clear criteria for marking, grading or otherwise giving certain specific kinds of feedback on students. But you may want to consider what time and other boundaries apply even in this setting. Does your written view on a supervisee have longstanding impact? Is it balanced by other course elements? Does it specify where you have reservations and where you do not? Both on training courses and in other settings you need to know such parameters for yourself and in order to be able to pass them on to supervisees.

So many are the permutations in which it is possible to supervise (according to setting, orientation, developmental match, hierarchical or cooperative contract and so on) that you are obliged to analyse carefully where the lines of your own responsibility lie. Let us take another example.

You are a member of a peer supervision group. One of the counsellors talks about a client with whom he appears to have a very close relationship. Indeed, the client is a young, vulnerable woman in need of considerable care, because she has a serious eating disorder. You are concerned that the client–counsellor relationship seems too intimate and also that your colleague has little experience with such serious problems. You voice your own concerns but no one agrees with you; they all consider that your colleague is working courageously and well. What will you do? Exactly what are your responsibilities in this case? To take it further, suppose that the client is subsequently admitted to hospital, is seriously ill and her parents begin to make angry enquiries about the counsellor and his accountability. Where do you stand? In our view, you should make clear your reservations in such a case, have them recorded, and urge colleagues to consider action. You may also need to consider withdrawing from such a group if your concerns receive no support.

It is impossible to anticipate every such eventuality, but what is clear is that if you have any supervisory responsibility at all, you should discover what the boundaries involved are. In some cases you may have difficulty deciding and colleagues may not be able to help you. This is certainly an instance where you need to consult with a senior colleague, even if only on a one-off basis. In certain cases it may be appropriate to consult your professional organization and even your insurance company. Many insurance companies offering treatment risk cover also cover supervisory responsibilities and sometimes provide a telephone 'hotline' for urgent enquiries which have implications for your own professional protection.

Key point

Clarify your position with regard to line managers, trainers, colleagues and anyone to whom you are accountable for your supervisory work, and do not underestimate the subtle areas in which boundaries may become dangerously blurred.

11

Utilizing a Variety of Supervisory Foci and Methods

7 Invite supervisees to engage in detailed case discussion

In Section 1 we discussed the usefulness of exchanging views with supervisees on the meaning and alternative ways of conducting supervision. Common to all approaches is a need for the supervisor to gain a certain amount of necessary information on each of the supervisee's clients. One of the obvious differences between counselling and supervision is that you, as the supervisor, usually do not meet the client, you do not know what they look like and indeed all you know about them is what your supervisee tells you and what you infer, more or less accurately. As a supervisor, you may sometimes find yourself somewhat hampered by discussing a shadowy, anonymous client figure. We believe that as supervisors we are entitled to as much information as we need in order to get a clear picture of the client, the client's functioning and any possible serious problems in counselling. Opinions vary (from counsellor to counsellor, supervisor to supervisor and orientation to orientation) as to whether, and how, counsellors should formally assess their clients.

What are the issues involved in intake and assessment procedures that supervisors need to consider? Some supervisors ask that certain details are always taken, for example name, address, date of birth, details of parents and siblings, medical and psychiatric history, present living circumstances, physical appearance, and so on. Others are concerned only with the strictly relevant details. Some insist on an intake assessment, others recommend delaying assessment until after a period of trial counselling has been undergone. Lukas (1993) gives many useful examples of what can and sometimes should be asked at the assessment stage. Lazarus (1989) provides an example of a thorough assessment format which is to be used judiciously rather than invariably. How you approach your supervisees with their new cases will depend on the setting in which you work, your own training background and theoretical orientation, your own clinical views and experience, and your own preferences. How supervisees present their case discussions will also depend on their wish to cooperate with or please you, their need to deal with several cases in a short time, their anxiety, and so on. See Appendix 1 for an example of how cases may be presented in supervision. Time permitting, you may be able to facilitate discussion of each of your supervisee's clients; alternatively, you and the supervisee may need to focus on those clients with more urgent or problematic issues. What is meant by case discussion? The term usually refers to the supervisee's verbal report about a client, often but not always supported by detailed notes. Many counsellors are taught to make process recordings after each session in which they record as accurately as they can what transpired within the session, the presumed interactional processes and their own impressions at the time and afterwards. Discussion of clients based on this model often concentrate on clients' problems, the counsellor's conceptualization of them, actual interventions and possible future strategies. A case discussion might include something like the following:

Supervisee: He's very depressed. He lives at home with his parents and is unemployed. He told me that he's 'fed up with everything' and can't see a way out. He was very monosyllabic in the session. I think he may be a suicidal risk.
Supervisor: Can you tell me a bit more about what his typical day is like – his behaviour – and the kinds of negative thought patterns he has?
Supervisee: He gets up late, doesn't eat much, manages to go for a walk, sees one or two friends. From the way he talks, I'd say he's thinking 'What's the point of carrying on? There's nothing in life for me, no one's interested in me.'
Supervisor: So he's not entirely inactive or isolated, that's good, isn't it? And it sounds like he has certain self-indoctrinating thoughts going on. What opinion have you formed about where you might go next with him?

The main focus here is at first on the client himself, his problem and its context, and it then turns to the subject of the counsellor's conceptualization and plans. This dialogue is based on the counsellor's perception and memory of what transpired and his personal and clinical impression of the client. The supervisor's concern is to know as much as necessary about the client and to help the counsellor focus on essentials. This approach varies according to theoretical orientation, of course, and a psychodynamic supervisor, for example, would probably elicit more details about the client–counsellor relationship and the client's childhood. The case discussion approach often takes a 'macro' perspective on supervision, which means that it relies on the supervisor's overall impression of the counsellor's selective report.

The macro perspective maintains a useful overview of what the counsellor is doing with a client and can certainly allow for various angles to be considered critically and creatively. When using this approach, explain its strengths and weaknesses to supervisees and seek their active collaboration in the process and its evaluation.

It is hard to imagine any supervision which does not include some case discussion or 'case-centred' work and some supervisors use it predominantly. In this Section on supervisory foci we are suggesting that it is beneficial to be familiar with and to practise a range of supervisory interventions. There are advantages and disadvantages to each of them. Case discussion is sometimes criticized for being overly focused on the remote 'nuts and bolts' of past sessions with the client, or for being based on a dry discussion of details remote from the vitality of the supervision session itself. This seems a rather unfair and almost unethical position when you remember that the central purpose of supervision is to protect and help the client.

A more serious objection to relying on case discussion entirely is its selectiveness. Both consciously and unconsciously, counsellors are probably inclined to attend to certain data and to neglect other material. By the time case notes are written (ideally immediately after the session, but often later) some material will have been forgotten altogether and certain parts will have been censored or conveniently forgotten because the counsellor failed to attend, could not understand or use them. Clinical notes are always likely to reflect to a considerable extent what the supervisee chooses to present. It has been demonstrated that process recordings are of dubious accuracy (Covner, 1944); Muslin et al., 1981). We do not mean here to impugn the reports or intentions of most supervisees; rather, it seems to be human nature that we perceive selectively and that such selective perception breeds yet further inaccuracy as it goes on, like Chinese whispers. As a possible corrective or counterbalance to case discussion, consider the merits of audio- and video-recording which, with their inevitable 'micro' perspective on counselling (entailing attention to small details within sessions), highlight the 'actual data' of counselling sessions. Goldberg (1985) discusses and compares the relative merits of process-, audio- and video-recordings and we recommend that you consider these when trying to establish a suitable balance for your own case discussions with supervisees.

Key point

Weigh up the merits and demerits of the case discussion approach, consider the elements which constitute productive case discussion and encourage supervisees to understand these.

---

8   Refer to parallel process issues when these are meaningful

Parallel process is described by Mattinson in the following terms: 'The processes at work currently in the relationship between client and worker are often reflected in the relationship between worker and supervisor' (1975: 11). It was Searles (1955) who first coined the term and described the phenomenon, which is sometimes confusingly referred to as a 'reflection process' and as 'mirroring'. (We say confusingly because these terms are used quite differently by other writers.) Mattinson refers to an 'unconscious mimicry' by the counsellor of the client, when discussing the client in supervision. While probably all counsellors understand and convey objectively much of their clients' material, it is argued that what is not consciously or objectively understood, especially in more difficult-to-understand (or 'disturbed') clients, often automatically transmits itself unconsciously. For this reason, many supervisors, and especially those with psychodynamic sympathies, identify and utilize parallel process phenomena in their work.

In parallel process or 'paralleling' within supervision, it is sometimes the case that an otherwise competent and clear-thinking counsellor may appear to be awkward and confused, or an otherwise well-balanced counsellor will become angry or depressed, when talking about a client. In group supervision, different group members may behave in particular, observable ways specifically in relation to hearing another group member describe a client. When a couple's problems are being presented in group supervision, it may be that some group members unconsciously identify with certain aspects of one partner and others with aspects of the other partner.

In order to work effectively with parallel process as a supervisor, you need to be highly aware of your own, subtly shifting inner states of mind and feeling. Although the humanistic and psychodynamic approaches obviously focus more on these states than do the cognitive and behavioural approaches, for example, it is not beyond the ability of any supervisor to become attuned to their own sensations, their own typical responses to supervisees, and to develop these so as to learn to discriminate between supervisees' normal behaviour and their behaviour when it is affected by certain clients. The art of working with parallel process is based partly on the willingness to accept it as a universal phenomenon (Doehrman, 1976). Doehrman claims that behaviours unconsciously duplicate themselves not only within supervision but also in reverse, from supervision back into the counselling relationship. She believes that these processes are always present in supervisory relationships and that they are ignored at our peril. Just as there is often some form of countertransference evident in all counselling relationships, so in supervision the supervisor's countertransference must be taken seriously. Contained within the countertransference there are often clues of a parallel process nature, which can be utilized or misunderstood.

Samuels talks about 'embodied countertransference' and 'reflective countertransference' (1989: 151). The latter refers to the kind of process we have been discussing. The former, however, refers to the unsettling experience within the counsellor (or supervisor, in our case) of 'an entity, theme, or person of a long-standing, intrapsychic, inner world nature'. In other words, the counsellor may pick up the client's current or chronic mood or condition (reflective countertransference) or, more deeply, may unconsciously pick up specific aspects of (or an uncanny sense of significant people from) the client's troubled past. Now, this may presumably happen in supervision too. If we are aware of our bodily and behavioural responses, our feeling responses and our fantasy responses to supervisees, we may be able to make fine (and relevant and usable) discriminations, to be fed back to supervisees. But how is this done? Some possible examples:

'I notice that as you are talking I am feeling quite distant from you. Is there something about your client that makes *you* feel that way?'

'As you have described your client's antics I have been getting angrier and angrier, yet there is nothing in your manner of anger, nor does your client appear to experience anger. Does this mean anything to you?'

'I am listening to you and at the same time I keep thinking of the edge of a cliff; the image keeps popping into my mind. I think there is something about the way you present your client that worries me.'

Sometimes such feedback strikes home, the supervisee may immediately make a conscious connection and find it very helpful. On occasion, supervisors being as fallible as anyone else, such comments may in fact be their own imagination or misplaced reflections. At yet other times, however, the feedback may have no immediate or obvious impact on the supervisee, yet may register unconsciously and find its way back into the counselling relationship, in the form of a delayed but still greater awareness of what the client is trying to express.

'This may mean nothing to you now – I'm not sure quite why it occurs to me – but I have a feeling about your client based on your (and now my) confusion, and I just want to say that I think she may have a problem that she is completely unaware of.'

This is the kind of intuitive, risky statement some supervisors are prepared to make from their trust in their own countertransference reactions. It is also the sort of statement which critics of the parallel process intervention may leap on.

We must confess that parallel process is not our major intervention in supervision and that we have reservations about it. Because it is an attractive idea (and, when it appears to work effectively, a dramatic one) it is often used far too indiscriminately, in our view. Pointing out parallel process can come to resemble a parlour game; some supervisors appear to watch out for it hawkishly and omnisciently announce its presence without checking out with supervisees whether they agree or understand; and because it appears to be 'deep', supervisees may be easily impressed and may compliantly accept the feedback, even when there is no truth in it whatsoever. Also, it can be used as one of the tools of the 'brilliant supervisor' whose interventions seem more calculated to demonstrate his or her own clinical wizardry than to help supervisees help clients. Another obvious problem with parallel process is that it does not readily fit some models of counselling. All supervisors should be aware of this phenomenon and should be able to utilize it when it is clearly in evidence and when it is likely to be a potent supervisory intervention. But like all other techniques, it can be over-used and used indiscriminately. One way of experimenting with it is to record your supervision sessions with particular emphasis on how you characteristically respond to each supervisee and compare this with exceptional responses. For example, 'I often find the time flies by in supervision with John, yet when we discussed his new client today, time went very slowly and I found myself irritated with John, without at the time knowing why.' Compare these reactions with the actual client material and ask yourself how different clients may be affecting your feelings towards your supervisees (and how these feelings, in turn, can be voiced usefully in supervision). Also, consult Doehrman (1976).

Key point

Learn to know when you may be detecting clues to your supervisees' clients' dynamics in the manner in which supervisees present their cases in supervision, and point out salient features of parallel process when it is helpful to do so.

---

9 Encourage the use of tape-recording

The tape-recording of counselling sessions remains a contentious subject. Although tape-recording has been used in the pioneering research of Carl Rogers and others for decades, considerable mistrust of and resistance to the practice is still evident. In this Section we intend to look at the practical concerns, the alleged ethical problems, the benefits and limitations of tape-recording and its uses in supervision.

We have argued previously (Dryden and Feltham, 1992) that the gains of tape-recording far outweigh any disadvantages and that the practicalities are easily mastered. If, as a supervisor, you already use and approve of taping, then you will not need to be convinced. If you are determined not to entertain the idea at all, we are unlikely to convince you. However, if you are considering using tapes and wish to know the issues involved, we begin with the subject of encouraging your supervisees to use tape-recording. We say 'encourage', but it has to be admitted that you may even insist, if you are a course tutor or course supervisor, on supervisees tape-recording their work. The rationale for insisting on the regular or occasional submission of supervisees' tapes is that this is probably the closest you can come to direct evidence of how supervisees actually work. Reliance on only their verbal reports of their own work is, we believe, unwise because (1) they cannot accurately or non-selectively recall details of interactions in sessions, (2) they are likely to distort, consciously or unconsciously, aspects of their work, especially if they are being assessed, and (3) verbal reports may favour the more articulate or artful of supervisees and discriminate against those who are inclined to discount their own strengths. There are also philosophical problems inherent in relying entirely on people's accounts of what they think they did as opposed to what you can witness for yourself (Ryle, 1949). This argument does not imply that supervisors should mistrust individual supervisees, but rather that they are well advised to consider the additional advantages of listening to tapes of actual counselling work.

You might also consider the following points when explaining the benefits of tape-recording to your supervisees. First, tape-recording explicitly demonstrates that the counsellor takes his or her work seriously enough to study it between sessions and together with a supervisor. The objection that direct recording breaches confidentiality is not valid, since counsellors take notes of sessions and report to supervisors anyway, and tape-recording is simply a technologically superior method of recording and of relaying the contents to a supervisor.

Second, in our experience and that of many of our colleagues, most clients have no objection to their sessions being tape-recorded and experience no interference from the process once it is established. What is common, however, is that supervisees who themselves object to, or who are afraid of, tape-recording, seem to convey their unease to clients, who then may refuse to have their sessions taped. Counsellors who are enthusiastic about tape-recording rarely experience such refusal.

Third, any client who objects or who shows any non-verbal anxiety about being tape-recorded, should have his or her feelings respected, without question. A small number of clients, for various reasons, do object, and this should always be accepted. All clients should have explained to them the purpose of tape-recording, the limits of its confidentiality (for example, that tapes will be played to supervisors or assessing tutors), that they will be safeguarded and duly destroyed when no longer needed.

Fourth, some counsellors play back parts of tape-recordings to their clients in sessions, or make copies of them for clients to take home and listen to. Part of the 'interpersonal process recall' method (Kagan, 1980) entails the 'mutual recall' of feelings that were unexpressed within sessions by both counsellor and client. Rusk (1991) advocates tape-recording for the sake of the client alone, in other words, the client is always given a tape of each session for their own study.

What are the actual supervisory uses of tape-recording? As we have indicated, material on tape gives you access to what the client and counsellor actually said to each other. (It does not, of course, convey body language, subtle gestures and what goes on during silences.) We find, on listening to tapes of clients after supervisees have already talked about them, that there are sometimes surprising discrepancies between how we and our supervisees perceive clients. For example, one supervisee described his client as 'hysterical', but when we heard her on tape she sounded simply like someone with a speech style that was fast and emotional, but with no real psychopathological undertones. Such examples do not imply that we are right and our supervisees are wrong, but that taped material can yield important discrepancies for discussion, and that these discrepancies may not come to light without tape-recording.

More importantly, counselling sessions on tape enable you and your supervisee to examine in as microscopic detail as you find helpful, every intervention the counsellor makes. This is particularly useful at the training stage when it is necessary for trainers and supervisors to monitor trainees' development closely and to be aware of any early, obvious problems. We might say here, in counter-argument to those who object to tape-recording on supposedly ethical grounds, that it might be considered unethical to allow trainees to qualify unless you have some very direct evidence of their competency with clients. We have argued (Dryden and Feltham, 1994a) that trainers too often rely on vague, inferential evidence of trainees' competency. Supervision of trainees' tapes does not have an inquisitorial function, but an intention to know what trainee counsellors are actually doing and to offer corrective guidance in those instances where they are clearly not working in clients' best interests.

There are various ways of using tapes in supervision. First, you may ask your supervisee to bring in and play specific parts of the work about which he or she has concerns and wishes to seek your views. This requires that the supervisee marks the places on the tape at which he or she wishes to stop it (by referring to the counter on the tape-recorder) and allows time for discussion of each significant section. Second, you may simply play through parts of a tape in order to get a flavour of the supervisee's work. You may, for instance, sample from the beginning, middle and end of a tape, in order to hear how the supervisee begins, structures and terminates a session. Similarly, the supervisee may wish to forward and re-wind the tape to moments and passages in the session which give a representative picture of his or her work. Third, you may on occasion listen to a complete tape. This is common practice on some counselling courses, where supervisors may have responsibility for detailed assessment and grading of tapes at the end of each year. You may also supervise entire tapes when a supervisee requests that you do so in order to give full feedback on a particular case or on the supervisee's skills at a particular stage in his or her development. You may also, in certain circumstances, supervise tapes sent by mail. Dryden (1991a) lists the possible reasons for such a practice (which include the geographical remoteness of some counsellors from supervisors, and seeking supervision from specialist practitioners who may even live in other countries) and the practical and ethical considerations involved.

We have both found useful Hill and O'Grady's (1985) list of therapist intentions when supervising and assessing trainees' tapes at Goldsmiths College and in other settings (see Appendix 3). This is a list of 19 clusters of purposeful counsellor behaviours which each demonstrate certain identifiable processes within sessions. Students, too, are helped by listening to their own tapes alongside some such guide which provides them with criteria for understanding what they were attempting to achieve in each session. Each theoretical orientation will suggest the items (skills, strategies, conceptualizations, relationship quality, etc.) that should be focused on in supervision of tapes.

Apart from certain individuals' objections to tape-recording, there are some drawbacks to be considered. Clear tape-recordings are needed, and this means that counsellors must obtain good equipment; it is usually necessary to obtain a good quality external microphone, for example. Counsellors need to practise using the equipment so that its operation does not distract from the work of the session at all. In listening to tapes, it is usually only possible to comment on short segments within any given supervision session, and there is a danger of concentrating too exclusively on the micro aspects of counselling, thus distorting the nature of the counselling relationship and its progress over time. There is sometimes an initial danger that counsellors want to 'perform' because they know their supervisor will be listening to the tape; this tends to disappear quite quickly, however. Particularly anxious trainees may find that tape-recording inhibits them and care obviously needs to be taken to help such trainees to overcome their anxiety. Explicit training in how to make tape-recordings, presenting their purpose to clients, resolving ethical dilemmas, and overcoming self-consciousness (for example, by repeated role-play and cognitive disputing), can help counsellor trainees enormously. Anticipate these difficulties, then, but do experiment with the use of tape-recording and incorporate its use into your supervisory practice. Consider, too, the practice of taping some of your own supervision sessions in order to improve your supervisory skills. Refer to Appendix 4 for examples of typical supervisor intentions and skills and use this when listening to tapes of your own supervisory sessions.

Key point

Take into account the advantages, disadvantages and various uses of tape-recording in supervision, encourage your supervisees to make tapes within an ethical framework and to learn from them with you and in their own self-supervision.

---

10 Focus on supervisees' specific strategies and interventions with each client

Case discussion and analysis of the counsellor–client relationship have an important place in supervision, but there is often a risk that counsellors' specific, moment-to-moment intentions within and across their sessions are overlooked. By this we mean that clients in fact present for counselling when they have a serious concern or problem to work on and counsellors therefore need to maintain an ongoing awareness of these concerns and direct their interventions to them purposefully. Counselling theory is a means to an end and, as Lazarus (1989) reminds us, clients are helped by what actually happens in sessions (and outside them) rather than by theory. There is still debate about the potent factors in counselling, with many believing non-specific factors (Frank, 1973) and relationship factors (Lambert et al., 1986), rather than any specific techniques or interventions, to be the 'active ingredients'. As a supervisor, you may be influenced strongly by such latter arguments and view your task accordingly, as helping your supervisees to improve their interpersonal sensitivity rather than their knowledge of specialized techniques or interventional skills.

Everything the counsellor says during a session may be considered an intervention. Lazarus (1989), in supervising his students, emphasizes the importance of the 'response-couplet'. He argues that for each statement made by the client, the counsellor must respond with a statement or question, and that each response may be regarded as neutral, positive or negative. Positive responses facilitate therapeutic movement and negative responses diminish therapeutic progress. Neutral responses may not diminish or enhance, but be requests for further information, admissions of not understanding, and so on. What is important is that every intervention can be examined in terms of what it added to the client's self-understanding, the therapeutic alliance and commitment to therapeutic action. You may ask yourself, and your supervisees, the following kinds of questions:

1 Did this intervention follow on from what the client was saying?
2 Was the purpose of this intervention understood by the client?
3 Was this intervention potent, delivered as it was at this particular time?
4 Was the intervention delivered skilfully (that is, was the way in which it was delivered – not only conceived – helpful to the client)?
5 Was the intervention phrased in such a way that the client could readily understand it (for example, was jargon avoided)?
6 Was the intervention followed through, rather than simply 'thrown in' casually?

It is, of course, difficult, if not impossible, to offer supervision of specific interventions without access to these in the form of tape-recordings, but to some extent supervisees can report some of their word-for-word interventions. It is easier to identify and examine strategies, or procedures which may span several sessions. What distinguishes moment-to-moment interventions from strategies is that the latter represent a purposeful 'macro' movement, consisting of a conceptualization and a 'treatment plan'. Strategies are not, however, necessarily understood as clinical step-by-step procedures by all counsellors. Here is an example:

Supervisee: My client describes herself as having panic attacks and I'm unsure how to handle this.

Supervisor: 'Panic attack' is her term, which you seem to see as a distinct and perhaps very challenging problem for you.

Supervisee: Yes. I have the idea that I should do something different or special, and I feel a bit inadequate.

Supervisor: So you're not saying that you find the client herself different but the concept of a panic attack concerns you. Can you tell me what you feel about the client herself?

Supervisee: Yes, I find her warm, friendly, perhaps rather conscientious. She seems nervous about me and about our sessions. I have the sense that she is afraid to assert herself and yet that she needs to. If she did more often, perhaps she wouldn't have what she calls panic attacks.

Supervisor: So you have a hunch that her fear of asserting herself perhaps produces these panic attacks in some way and that even in your sessions there is some evidence of her withholding her assertiveness?

Supervisee: Yes, and I feel as if she's kind of pushing me to tell her that she comes across in this way, and I think that if I tell her what impact she makes on me, that may be the start of her understanding how she builds her own foundations for panic.

Words like 'strategy' do not appear here, but it is evident that the supervisee has intuitively formulated a hypothesis about the client, along with a sense of what may prove helpful to the client in future sessions. This is, of course, a strategy of sorts. In this example, the supervisor might, in a later supervision session, follow up on whether and how the supervisee put his hunches into practice. In other words, an attempt might be made to identify specific interventions, exactly how they were made, and whether they were timely and effective.

Hill and O'Grady (1985/Appendix 3) offer a list of key intentions which can be used in supervision to help identify what the supervisee had in mind during sessions with clients. Using this schema is easier when tapes of actual sessions are used in supervision, but even without tapes it is a useful guide and reminder of what has been attempted in counselling. Hill et al. (1988) researched clients' awareness of and reactions to counsellors' interventions. Given a very little help in identifying key counsellor interventions, clients were subsequently able to rate the helpfulness of their counsellors' interventions. This research suggests that clients were acutely aware and appreciative of counsellors' intentions to 'support' and 'instil hope', for example, but that they had less positive reactions to intentions to 'promote insight' or to 'gather information'. Most significantly, Hill et al. found that counsellors often failed to identify accurately their clients' reactions to their interventions, and often proceeded to further interventions without realizing that this failure had occurred. While we acknowledge that not all supervision can or should focus on microscopic interactions and interventions, it seems to us that this aspect of supervision should never be entirely omitted, particularly from the work of beginning counsellors. Even in the work of the 'master practitioner', detailed attention to counsellor intentions, interventions and strategies is likely to prove very rewarding.

A final argument for the value of giving attention to these detailed aspects of actual interventions is illustrated by Strozier et al. (1993). Using and adapting the Hill and O'Grady (1985) list of therapist intentions, Strozier and her colleagues closely studied and mapped a single supervisory relationship, identifying supervisor intentions and the degree to which these were understood and found helpful by the supervisee. 'Exploratory' and 'restructuring' interventions were found to be most helpful. The reflective supervisor will, we believe, benefit from studying his or her own interventions and strategies in and across sessions and will model to supervisees the importance of maintaining a close watch on the impact of interventions. This mode of supervision serves to demystify the counselling process, to bring into the open what counsellors and supervisors consciously think they are doing and to examine the correlation between specific interventions and strategies and their success or otherwise.

Key point

Focus closely on supervisees' and your own detailed intentions, actions and strategies within and across sessions, and learn from them what is effective and what is not.

11   Encourage supervisees to brainstorm, role-play and use other catalytic aids to understand their clients

Getting into an impasse with clients is a far from uncommon experience. There are many causes of 'stuckness', including the client's fear, depression, lack of energy, or inability to collaborate, or the counsellor's fear or skill deficits, or a combination of client and counsellor factors. Sometimes a counselling relationship which begins with crisis and energy runs down into a plodding, safe and uncreative affair. Sometimes the client may appear quite contented with the level of progress but the counsellor is left feeling that little is happening, or is left confused. Sometimes these are manifestations of transference and countertransference dynamics. But it is also the case, we believe, that counsellors can become tired, confused or lost for far less 'dynamic' reasons. In brief counselling, for example (Dryden and Feltham, 1992), counsellors may not have the luxury of allowing the client to lapse into long silences and totally unproductive sessions. It is in the nature of certain counselling contracts that counsellors are called on to be exceptionally alert and creative. But even having obtained the client's agreement to work in a focused manner, it can still happen that the client will lose commitment, become confused or fearful, or that the counsellor will 'run out of steam'. It also happens that energy or focus may be lost in supervision and that here too it can become useful to consider alternative methods for enlivening and bringing fresh focus to the work.

Brainstorming

Brainstorming is often associated with team or group meetings but may also be used to great effect in individual counselling and supervision. Variations on brainstorming or divergent thinking lie at the heart of many innovative approaches in counselling and therapy, such as neuro-linguistic programming and solution-focused brief therapy. Egan (1990) recommends this form of divergent thinking and suggests the following steps in the process, which we have adapted to apply to the supervisory situation:

1 Suspend your judgement and encourage supervisees to suspend theirs. Create the kind of free climate in which you and your supervisee can play with ideas in relation to certain clients. 'Well, I couldn't possibly do that with my client', is exactly the kind of judgemental statement that is to be discouraged in this exercise, although it may well apply at many other times.

2 Encourage supervisees to generate as many ideas and strategies as possible. Do not allow your supervisees lamely to suggest one or two ideas but enthusiastically prompt them to come up with more. 'I can't think of anything else', might be countered with, 'Are you sure about that? Remember that this exercise is about free thinking. Give me two or three more ideas – anything that springs to mind.'

3 Help supervisees to use one idea as a springboard to another. Enter the spirit of brainstorming and encourage a creative 'free association' exercise in the sense of rich, lateral thinking ultimately aimed at helping the client. For example, 'I could ask my client to take me to her mother's house and show me exactly what is so irritating about her mother . . . and I could invite my client to my house and show her how I deal with my mother's irritating ways!'

4 Challenge supervisees to produce usefully zany ideas. Remember again that this is a supervisory exercise. You are not suggesting to your supervisee that he or she starts to act zanily in counselling sessions (although some approaches do countenance apparent zaniness!). 'I'd like to send my client off to the Amazon . . . . I'd like the pair of us to spend a week in a sauna.' At this stage, the ideas and images do not have to make sense (or be politically correct!); indeed, it is better if they are not sensible.

5 Help your supervisees to clarify what they have produced. Ask questions designed to gain more detailed pictures and information in relation to each thought and image, thus encouraging vividness and motivation. You might ask, 'And how would you feel in the sauna, what would you talk about together?'

In suspending 'normal' supervisory conventions, you enable the supervisee to gain valuable new perspectives on their cases. Often the exercise will dislodge some of the stuckness. It may promote catharsis, allowing a supervisee to experience exactly how difficult a certain client is, or how problematic a certain aspect of countertransference is. Sometimes promising new strategies will be generated.

Role-play

'Talking about' is usually the main instrument in supervision, even when feelings and subtle parallel processes are under consideration. It is sometimes useful to switch from this conversational mode to one of enactment and experience. There are various ways of role-playing aspects of counselling in order to experience and work on new perspectives of cases. We look at some of these:

1 Ask the supervisee to play the part of the client in question. As the supervisor, you become the counsellor, and attempt to work in your own way with the client's material. This allows the supervisee to experience the client's perspective and it allows the supervisor a vivid presentation of the client. It also recreates, in many complex ways, the difficulties there may be between client and counsellor and between supervisee and supervisor.

2 Ask the supervisee to role-play a client. This time, as the supervisor you become a researcher. You ask the 'client' questions about the counselling and the counsellor. For example, 'How well do you think your counselling is progressing? How clearly do you think your counsellor understands your concerns? If there is any one thing you would like your counsellor to do differently, what would it be?' This exercise forces the supervisee into the client's frame of reference and allows him or her to consider fresh angles on how he or she is working with a particular client.

3 Ask the supervisee to role-play both him- or herself and the client, alternately. To make this more vivid, consider the use of different chairs, so that the supervisee has to move physically as well as imaginally into the position of the client and counsellor. The supervisee may play the counselling relationship as it is perceived to be, or exaggerate parts of it in order to gain a better understanding, or change parts in order to experiment in a brainstorming sense. The supervisee might, thus, shout at the client, 'I'm sick of you sitting there expecting me to do all the work. You've spent your whole life just waiting for others to rescue you!'

4 Ask the supervisee to role-play the supervisor (either you as he or she perceives you, or another, highly critical supervisor or a supervisor with X-ray vision). This exercise allows the supervisee to enter into his or her own fantasies about the counselling work, how it is perceived and what its worst, or best, features may be. This can also allow for greater insight into the supervisory alliance.

The supervisor needs to give clear support and permission for all these exercises, because they can be very powerful, can lead to dramatic insights and feelings, and may feel threatening to some supervisees. They are not an end in themselves but should be used purposefully to help supervisees gain new ideas and consider new strategies. Hence, ample time for discussion should be provided within the supervision session. Remember to de-role supervisees who use these role-plays.

Depending on the setting in which you work, there is a variety of catalytic exercises and aids that you may call upon. If you supervise in a group, for example, you can utilize other group members to play parts of the counsellor and client relationship. You may ask one member to 'be' the client's sullenness, another to enact the part of the client's wife, yet another to be the 'stuck' counsellor, and so on. This kind of exercise perhaps comes more naturally to Gestalt and other humanistic counsellors but can be adapted. Another example is a rational role reversal applied to supervision. This is from the repertoire of rational emotive behaviour therapy (Dryden, 1982) and requires the supervisor to take the part of the supervisee who is irrationally disturbed in his or her work; the supervisee, taking the part of the supervisor, then disputes the irrational thinking involved and helps to establish a rational perspective (for example, 'There is no evidence that I *must* be able to help this client overcome his sexual dysfunction'). Such exercises should always be adapted according to the theoretical orientation and developmental stage of the supervisee.

Key point

Consider the advantages of using certain catalytic exercises which may enable supervisees to gain new and useful perspectives on particularly problematic cases, and ensure that such exercises are explained, used purposefully and that suitable de-briefing methods are employed.

12 Consider the relative advantages and disadvantages of individual, group and peer supervision

Many counsellor training courses recommend that trainees receive a mixture of individual and group supervision. Such a mixture exposes trainees to the intensive attention of individual supervision and the many challenges of group supervision. It also begins to teach them about the relative merits of these two forms of supervision. But compromises are often involved in these matters and supervisees may find themselves in one or other of these settings not from choice but because alternatives are not practicable. Supervisees may go through an entire training with very little individual supervision because it is too expensive to provide, for example. We propose here to examine the advantages and disadvantages of individual, group and peer supervision, all of which have merits and problems and all of which are endorsed as valuable by the BAC (see Appendix 2).

Individual supervision

In one-to-one supervision, the following benefits are apparent:

1 The supervisee and supervisor can decide and work on an agenda without any distraction.
2 There is time for discussion of the supervisee's cases in every session.
3 There is an opportunity to examine closely the progress of the supervisee's work with individual clients and to focus closely on the relationship between supervisee and supervisor.
4 One-to-one supervision duplicates the one-to-one nature of most counselling and hence provides useful modelling.
5 The supervisor can be reasonably sure that he or she has an overview of the supervisee's total caseload.
6 There is a high degree of confidentiality.

The following disadvantages may be apparent:

1 The supervisee receives the input of only one other person, which may sometimes be unhelpfully biased.
2 Supervisor and supervisee may share the same views too closely and thus unconsciously develop a collusive relationship.
3 The supervisee does not have the opportunity to compare his or her work with other counsellors, particularly those at the same developmental stage.

Just how advantageous individual supervision may be to each supervisee depends on a variety of factors. When there is an especially productive supervisory alliance, this can prove the most fruitful learning experience in the development of many counsellors (Norcross and Guy, 1989). The matching of theoretical orientations, congruence of personalities or complementarity of personalities, as well as goodness of fit between respective developmental stages, may all constitute a good supervisory alliance. Beginning supervisees may feel usefully supported, nurtured and tutored by a very experienced supervisor. Alternatively, they may sometimes benefit from supervision from a colleague who is not much more experienced than themselves and who is still struggling with identical issues.

Group supervision

In group supervision, the following benefits are apparent:

1 There is a great deal of stimulation and variety of perspectives on each supervisee's cases.
2 There is an opportunity to learn from the ways in which fellow supervisees handle their own counselling work.
3 Supervisees have the opportunity to hear about and learn from colleagues' work with a wide variety of clients.
4 The variety of views may act as a corrective against the single supervisor's biases or blindspots.
5 Group supervision may be very economical in training settings, in voluntary counselling organizations, or for those supervisees whose counselling work does not pay them very much.
6 The make-up of the group may provide useful opportunities for role-plays to be experimented with.

The following disadvantages may be apparent:

1 There may be insufficient time for each supervisee's concerns to be addressed in any detail.
2 Supervisees may have too much opportunity to 'hide' or to minimize their difficulties.
3 Supervisees may consciously or unconsciously compete with or thwart each other, particularly when supervised together in a training setting.
4 The variety of perspectives on each supervisee's cases may be experienced as a bombardment of conflicting and unhelpful views.
5 Group dynamics may become at times more distracting or interesting than the actual cases under discussion.
6 Confidentiality is somewhat less protected.

We have assumed that group supervision may be either supervised by someone appointed to the role from outside the group (for example, a supervisor on a training course), by a functional supervisor who may be elected or rotated each week from among the group members, or by all group members collectively. Each of these scenarios has its strengths and weaknesses. What they all have in common is a distinct difference from one-to-one supervision in which there are clear roles. Even in those cases where there is an appointed group supervisor, that person has different tasks from those faced by the supervisor in individual supervision. As a group supervisor, you may have to provide leadership, time management, interpretation of group dynamics, conflict resolution and other demanding functions. It is advisable that anyone undertaking the role of group supervisor should have previous experience and training in group dynamics, group therapy and group supervision. In spite of the challenges to be encountered, however, group supervision can be an exciting opportunity for exploring effective and new ways to work with clients, and most of the same skills can be used from individual supervision. The identification of and insight from parallel process, for example, can be achieved in groups, often with fascinating multiple parallels.

A problematic feature of group supervision is the division and sufficiency of time. The BAC recognizes the value of group supervision but argues that it must provide individual supervisees with adequate time and attention for their caseload. This means a minimum individual equivalent of one-and-a-half hours of supervision a month, but when supervisees have rather high caseloads this may need to be much more. A guideline figure is that counsellors-in-training should receive the equivalent of not less than one hour of weekly supervision for every eight clients (BAC, 1990). The British Psychological Society suggests a figure of one to five (BPS, 1993). (It is interesting to note that some American states specify a minimum of one, two or even four hours weekly supervision for post-Master licensure applicants and some states ask for more than 50 per cent of supervision to be individual rather than group in kind.) If you are providing group supervision, then, you need to consider carefully any ethical and organizational issues which bear on the adequacy of individual time for supervisees. How much time is available depends too on the size of each supervision group and how long it runs. A typical supervision group within a counselling training course lasts for two hours and contains three or four members. Many supervisors prefer two or three supervisees at most, but it is not unknown for supervisees to find themselves in far larger groups. It is difficult to see how groups of more than five or six can function adequately, allowing each supervisee sufficient time, particularly for urgent cases.

Peer supervision

In peer supervision, the following benefits are apparent:

1 Any dis-empowering aspects of supervision as provided by an 'expert' are minimized.
2 Participants can organize supervision meetings at their own convenience.
3 Payment can be avoided.
4 Participants may have high levels of understanding and support for each other's developmental stage and needs.
5 For very experienced counsellors, peer supervision may be the 'supervision of choice'.

The following disadvantages may be apparent:

1 No one has any final authority or clear mandate, for example to report any unprofessional behaviour.
2 Participants may avoid confronting each other when it is necessary to do so.
3 Participants may lack elements of necessary experience and expertise.
4 Participants may either collude with each other or lack the structure and skills to offer emotional containment to each other.

You may consider using peer supervision, either in a one-to-one or a group format. This is usually not recommended for beginners because a certain degree of supervisory experience is often called for in a trainee's early development, and also because it can be difficult for trainees of equal status to confront each other when necessary. But peer supervision is economical and it is sometimes the only practicable form of supervision, for example for counsellors living in remote areas where no supervisors are available. More experienced counsellors, who may be supervisors themselves, often make use of consultative support. In the USA and among many psychoanalysts in the UK, the preferred (and ethically acceptable) form of supervision is occasional consultation with senior colleagues when confronted with particularly difficult or unusual cases. This is often a good additional form of supervision for British counsellors but BAC considers it unethical for counsellors, no matter how experienced, to have less than the nominal one-and-a-half hours of formal supervision each month. Supervisors need to be particularly alert, perhaps, to the kinds of negotiations that colleagues may enter into with them, if these appear to erode accepted ethical standards.

In developing your own practice as a supervisor, you may wish to consider what the advantages and disadvantages are for you in offering individual, group and other forms of supervision. Your personal style and theoretical orientation may lend itself more to the special challenge of group supervision, or to the careful, detailed work involved in individual supervision. (We are not suggesting that these descriptions typify each of these formats!) Depending on your work setting, you may have little realistic choice, in which case you may need to consider how you can improve and extend your skills. It is possible that you might decide, for example, that group supervision is not for you and that you will either argue the case to supervise everyone individually, or to refer some of your staff or supervisees to a group elsewhere.

Key point

Examine what individual, group, peer and other forms of supervision have in their favour, what problems they may involve, what challenges these pose for you and how you might broaden your skills in each supervisory format.

Fostering and Using
the Supervisory
Relationship

13 Monitor and address the relationship between you and your supervisees

In initiating an effective supervisory alliance, part of the agreement between you and supervisees is likely to have centred on open communication. Explicit contracting encourages both parties to express any doubts, questions or challenges. You may have suggested to supervisees at the outset, for example, that you welcome their feedback on your supervision at any time and perhaps especially at review sessions. Supervisees know the importance of creating and maintaining a healthy relationship with their own clients and will expect this same awareness in their supervisors. However, beginning counsellors in particular may be reluctant to voice any doubts or criticisms. You may be perceived as an all-knowing and invariably correct authority, with the power to assess and fail. You yourself, depending on your own level of experience as a supervisor, may be unaware of the influence you exert on supervisees. You may be somewhat anxious about how you are perceived as performing. Unconsciously, there can be a temptation to act into the role of the wise and infallible supervisor, for example, especially if you feel threatened by your own lack of experience. Kadushin (1968) has pointed out that the field of supervision is rich in opportunities for gameplaying, and this can include supervisors as well as supervisees.

While some of what transpires between supervisor and supervisee may have direct clinical significance (for example, the identification and working through of parallel process), certain indirect relationship factors may become obstacles to the ultimate goal of helping the client. These need to be addressed so that they do not become obstructive. What kinds of obstacles are common? In the counselling relationship there may be an inadvertent mismatch between client and counsellor, based on personality traits, gender, race, sexual orientation, cultural and class factors (see Dryden and Feltham, 1994b). There are good reasons to suppose that there are far greater opportunities for such mismatches in supervisory relationships, in view of the relatively small number of supervisors practising and the fact that many supervisees have little or no choice of supervisor. Conn (1993) discusses some of the gender issues in supervision, for example the fact that managers and senior practitioners are still more often men than women and that when they supervise women, they are likely to transport patriarchal attitudes into the supervisory relationship. Counsellors in private practice, or trainees paying for their own supervision, are in a better position to choose, since they can shop around in the same way clients are encouraged to.

For these reasons, it is necessary that you are alert to possible tensions and conflicts in your relationship with supervisees. Because there is often a perceived or real difference of power between you, the supervisee may suppress anxieties or questions for fear of being judged or seen as lacking in competency. The supervisee may unwittingly relate to you as an infallible senior practitioner, which may reinforce your sense that you are working well, even when this may not be the case. There is much scope within supervision for transferential and countertransferential reactions, which should not go unaddressed if they threaten to interfere with the work. Supervisors from the person-centred tradition might prefer to view such issues as relating to supervisor and supervisee congruence (Mearns, 1991). Mearns outlines the many possibilities in the 'unspoken relationship':

1 Unclarified differences of opinion about the aims and practice of counselling and supervision.
2 The counsellor's unvoiced reactions to the supervisor.
3 The supervisor's unvoiced reactions to the counsellor.
4 The counsellor's unexpressed assumptions about the supervisor.
5 The supervisor's unexpressed assumptions about the counsellor.
6 The counsellor's unexpressed assumptions about how the supervisor experiences the counsellor's behaviour.
7 The supervisor's unexpressed assumptions about how the counsellor experiences the supervisor's behaviour.

There are layers upon layers of potential misunderstanding here. In a study of what was unexpressed between clients and counsellors (Regan and Hill, 1992) it was found that there were often wide discrepancies between assumptions and realities and that negative reactions in particular were often unexpressed, thus jeopardizing the therapeutic alliance. In supervision, there may be an assumption that an overriding concern for the client's material makes the maintenance of the supervisory relationship secondary. There may be an anxiety about converting supervision into counselling, leading to your ignoring any discussion of possible transference and countertransference. A strong supervisory alliance, however, is one in which it is recognized that at any moment, from session to session, and particularly in review sessions, it may be useful and necessary to focus on relationship obstacles. Consider the following examples.

Andrew is a beginning supervisor and his supervisee, Ben, is unaware of this. Both of them are anxious about their performance. Ben seeks reassurance that his work with clients is acceptable and often asks for specific advice on what he considers difficult problems. Andrew, anxious to be helpful and to win the approval of Ben and of his own supervisor, finds himself getting into knots. One moment he is giving Ben exactly the kind of supervision he seems to need, and the next moment ('kicking himself' for 'doing the supervisee's work for him') he withdraws. Ben becomes confused by this switching of styles.

How should such an obstacle be addressed? Who should initiate the process of reflecting on the difficulties? In this case, of course it would have been preferable if this scenario had not arisen, but since it has, here is a possible way forward:

Andrew: I would like to take some time to look at something which may be getting in the way between us. You seem to want quite a bit of direction from me and at times that may be appropriate, but perhaps if I become too directive it may prevent you from finding your own way forward. I may be tempted to give you the answers you want because of my own anxieties in supervising.

Ben: No, I think I appreciate your help with things where I really don't have the experience, but maybe sometimes I don't stop to think more for myself. I didn't realize, though, that there was any anxiety in this for you.

Andrew: Yes. You see, I haven't long been supervising and I should have made that clear at the outset. I have quite a lot of experience as a counsellor.

Ben: I've always found you very insightful and obviously very in touch with clients' feelings. I didn't ask about your experience as a supervisor, but thank you for telling me now.

This kind of dialogue could be more difficult, but here is an example of the supervisor's disclosure proving to be less painful or negative than feared by him. Indeed, in this example, the overt disclosure and concern begins to improve the supervisory relationship.

Sarah is an experienced counsellor who, as part of a further training, is obliged to receive supervision from Charles, who is considerably older than she is and apparently quite rigid and persecutory in his views. Sarah senses that supervision is not going as well as it might, but she has no choice of supervisor. Charles regards Sarah as being rather vague, undisciplined and careless in frame management. They are half way through a year together and there is a danger of Sarah failing the supervision component.

How is this impasse to be resolved? Sarah has assumed that she was having difficulties with the new approach in her course, but she begins to think it may be more to do with Charles's personality. With the possibility of failing growing real, she decides to take a risk:

Sarah: This is a bit hard for me, but I need to say that I'm concerned these sessions are not going well.

Charles: Please say some more about this.

Sarah: Well, I don't quite know what it is but we don't seem to get on very well. When I've had supervision before it's felt like I've had more space. Here, I feel as if I have to toe the line. I've wondered if that's because of this training, but I'm not so sure it is.

Charles: Well, I have felt something of the same sort between us. I think you are somewhat resistant to the training but perhaps I am reacting to you too.

Again, we are portraying a conversation that begins to improve communication, with both parties being reasonably willing to hear the other. In this example, it might be the case that Charles would not agree with Sarah's evaluation and might rather see her as wholly responsible for the misalliance. Although this is unlikely in mature and responsive supervisors, it is possible for some supervisors to become very set in their ways and resistant to new ideas or to energetic, younger counsellors. These are just two examples and there are obviously myriad possibilities for mis-communication in supervision. In order to minimize instances of misalliance, ensure that initial contracting encourages and even demands a high level of clear and honest, ongoing mutual feedback.

Key point

Be alert to the many ways in which you and your supervisees may fail to relate optimally and, being mindful of discrepancies in power, initiate and maintain a process of ongoing feedback.

14 Negotiate and implement evaluative review sessions

You may be seeing a particular supervisee weekly, fortnightly or monthly, under conditions that explicitly require evaluation or not. Your supervisee may have anything from one client to 20 or 30. Often, in the business of responding to ongoing, difficult and urgent cases, it seems that there is barely time to help the supervisee with an overview of his or her ongoing clients, let alone take time out to review his or her own development and the relationship between you. Yet without some mechanism for standing back and getting a perspective on supervision, there is a danger that the working alliance (Bordin, 1983) will be weakened and the supervisee's work undervalued. Furthermore, as Davis comments, 'Evaluation occurs whether or not it is made explicit or formalized. On balance there are advantages to formal and reciprocal evaluation procedures' (1989: 36).

Your initial contract may have included the suggestion that, 'From time to time, say every three months, I'd like us to devote a session to standing back and reflecting on your progress in your work and our progress together.' Of course it is quite unlikely that any supervisee would disagree, but when the time comes for an actual review session it may be another matter. There are apparently always urgent cases to discuss and no time for reviews! Close to the time you have agreed, remind the supervisee about the review, gain consent to use the next session, say, for this purpose, and invite the supervisee to consider his or her own agenda for it. What are some of the items that you and the supervisee might want to raise?

First could be 'How am I getting on?' Beginning counsellors are frequently anxious or concerned about their progress and may have an implicit question in mind ('Am I any good at counselling?'). Clear feedback is particularly necessary for beginning supervisees, since they may derive most of their sense of professionally 'good enough' competence from the supervisor's feedback. It is possible, if you adhere too closely to case material, to help supervisees significantly with their cases without, however, giving them a sense of their own strengths and deficits. Also, beginning supervisees often wish to know if they are putting their theoretical learning to good use and are 'going in the right direction'. Supervision is of paramount importance for such feedback.

A second item could be 'How are we getting on?' This question is more likely to be raised by the supervisor. It is good practice to raise it very early in your work with each supervisee (say, at the fourth, fifth or sixth session) and then to refer to it from time to time, and especially at formal review sessions. This question refers to the working alliance and whether there are sufficiently strong and shared bonds, goals and tasks (Bordin, 1983). 'Do we have a healthy rapport?'; 'Are we trying to achieve the same ends in supervision?'; 'Are the approaches we are using in supervision equally understood and valued by both of us?' These are salient areas to explore. You might ask more detailed questions, such as 'Are you finding that our original contract still holds or does it need to be adjusted in any way?' or 'When I asked you to "put the client on the chair and tell him how you feel", was that useful for you, or not?' or 'I have the impression that sometimes you may have certain things you'd like to raise but perhaps you don't feel you can – is there anything in that?' One way of gaining detailed information on the supervisee's perception of the quality of supervision is to use a comprehensive questionnaire such as Bernard and Goodyear's (1992), which is designed to elicit supervisees' views on their supervisors.

A third item could be 'What have been the major concerns in supervision?' This question addresses recurring themes. Both supervisee and supervisor are free to bring their own views on what constitutes the most important, pressing or recurring issues. Each person's view may be different. For example, the supervisee may say 'Well, my main concern is whether I'm remaining in the client's frame of reference', while the supervisor's may be 'I'm mainly concerned about your apparent reluctance to challenge when necessary'. More problematically, the supervisee's main concern may be the number of supervised hours he or she can accrue in a certain period, and yours may be a concern with the supervisee's unrecognized countertransference issues. Major concerns may be negative or positive, and supervisee and supervisor may share the same concerns or find themselves somewhat at odds. Conflict is perhaps less likely between mature practitioners, when the seasoned counsellor is aware of specific areas he or she wishes to focus on (Goldberg, 1992).

These are major agenda items for a review and are somewhat global in nature. Another approach is to evaluate detailed aspects of the supervisee's work. Particularly in the early stages of a counsellor's development, you may wish to negotiate a contract for close examination of the supervisee's work, for example by studying tape-recordings and transcripts, followed by a rigorous evaluation of the internalization of skills and application of theory. This kind of exercise is difficult to execute without recourse to questionnaires or other forms of written evaluation. Bradley (1989) gives many examples of the kinds of items that need to be raised in this exercise. Davis (1989) gives a simplified outline based on supervisees' conceptual ability, clinical performance and personal learning. Typical items are the counsellor's understanding and use of counselling skills and strategies, case conceptualizations, theoretical considerations, ethical and professional boundaries. Counsellors may be asked to rate themselves but your own evaluation of them may well have great weight, particularly if you are an assessing supervisor. You may choose to conduct a comparative evaluative exercise, measuring supervisees' own ratings against your own and subsequently discussing any discrepancies in your views. Certain items are extremely difficult to assess meaningfully when you have no direct evidence of the counsellor's skills, for example. A more difficult exercise still is to gather information from clients on their evaluation of counsellors (Hope, 1989).

When working with somewhat experienced counsellors (those referred to by Hawkins and Shohet (1989) as apprentice and journeyperson (see Section 4)), you may find it helpful to negotiate with them what level and kind of evaluation they would appreciate. There is no precise obligation for the counsellor in private practice, supervised by a supervisor in private practice, to engage in regular, formal, written evaluation exercises but it is good practice to review development and competence in some form. The supervisee may find it helpful to offer an audiotape of a full session to the supervisor for comprehensive analysis and commentary on his or her work, for example. Alternatively, the supervisee may submit a detailed case study to the supervisor. Naturally, suitable arrangements should be made for the supervisor to be reimbursed for any time spent on such evaluative supervision.

Reviews are a two-way process (indeed, in some ways they are always a three-way process, with the client at the heart of the matter) and you may, as a supervisor, wish to elicit formal feedback from supervisees on your work. You may rely on the verbal feedback given by supervisees and on your own supervisor's or consultants's feedback. An alternative method is to use questionnaires with your supervisees. One advantage of this method is that it overcomes to some extent supervisees' reluctance to give you negative verbal evaluation. Another is that it provides a systematic and detailed account of supervisees' reactions. Hart (1982) and Borders and Leddick (1987) offer examples of such questionnaires. When you use these, it is important to give permission and encouragement to supervisees to be candid and also to follow up on the evaluation where it is indicated that you may need to improve certain areas of your supervision. This exercise obviously requires a highly non-authoritarian approach. Indeed, it is crucial to the entire atmosphere of review sessions that both parties respect each other's right to give constructive feedback. Houston emphasizes that 'a review is not about the bolstering of complacency, nor yet about the tidy apportioning of blame' (1990: 90).

Key point

Contract with supervisees to hold periodic review sessions which allow opportunities for meaningful feedback in both directions, and use whatever evaluative instruments best address developmental or assessment needs.

---

15 Allow supervisees to express and explore negative feelings about clients and about counselling in general

So powerful are the images contained in the idea of supervision that many counsellors believe that they must always take the business of supervision very seriously, must always present their work conscientiously and must never reveal any doubts about their suitability for the work. This is, we would argue, quite unrealistic. No counsellor can love or like all clients, enjoy all counselling sessions or sail through the activity of counselling without giving some thought to its stresses, aggravations and negative aspects.

Beginning counsellors have an especially difficult experience, since they are often supervised by people who are assessing them, they are often anxious about their competency and about what lies before them as a career choice. But all counsellors may encounter particularly challenging clients or low times in their career. Here, we look at several common difficult elements in counsellors' experience of counselling and how these may emerge in supervision.

1 Counsellors are taught the importance of non-judgementalism but sometimes find themselves working with clients whose behaviour borders on the unacceptable.
2 Counsellors have vulnerabilities of their own and may sometimes meet clients by whom they feel too threatened to work with productively.
3 Some clients are poorly motivated and offer very little for counsellors to work with.
4 There are times in counselling with individual clients or with a whole caseload, when the counsellor has little sense of progress, which may be construed as demoralizing.
5 It is not until counsellors become involved in the work that they realize its joys, challenges and stresses.
6 Counsellors may become overwhelmed by the pain of certain clients or client groups.
7 Counsellors may undergo difficulties in their own lives which temporarily make the work particularly taxing for them.
8 Particular clients sometimes 'get to' counsellors, 'get under their skin', because of certain countertransference factors.

Undoubtedly, some of these issues need to be addressed in the personal counselling of the counsellor. However, some of them are issues of professional development, organizational and case management, parallel process and projective identification and other conceptual issues which may hold keys to helping or protecting clients. Section 3 examined some of these boundaries, but here we wish to focus on the legitimate use of supervision for what Inskipp and Proctor (1989) call restoration. It cannot be presupposed that all emotional reactions to the stresses and challenges of counselling are indicative of the personal psychopathology of the counsellor. Counselling is often stressful (Dryden and Varma, 1994) and part of the supervisor's role is to monitor the impact of stress on supervisees. As a supervisor, you can help your supervisees to discriminate between the phenomena of projective identification (in which the counsellor is 'made to' experience some of the feelings or dynamics of the client); client–counsellor mismatches (where it is likely that the client should be referred elsewhere); unhelpful countertransference on the part of the counsellor (requiring exploration or further therapy); too high a caseload (indicating a need for an adjustment by the counsellor and/or the counsellor's manager); and severe stress and burnout (which may suggest a need for temporary or permanent withdrawal from working as a counsellor).

Let us consider an example. Marjorie is working with a depressed young man who she has seen for a year. The counselling seems not to be getting anywhere. She has tried 'staying with the stuckness' and has also tried some task-setting, but all apparently to no avail. She also has three or four other similar clients. Her personal life is problematic, in that her father died a few months ago and her current relationship with her partner is poor. She is a dedicated counsellor and has had a lengthy experience of her own therapy in the past. The supervisor believes that she will pull through her present struggles and offers her a great deal of support. Marjorie appears to be able to discriminate between her own concerns and the depression of a few clients. Yet she cannot help complaining about this particular client: 'He's just really getting me down and I wish I could get rid of him.'

How might the supervisor intervene here? Knee-jerk supervisory reactions might include a strong suggestion that Marjorie re-enters personal therapy, that she analyse the relationship between her own bereavement, current relationship and difficult (male) client, or even that she terminates her counselling with this client and refers him elsewhere. But how else might the supervisor help?

Supervisor: You've had a hard time of your own lately, yet in spite of that you've given Anthony a caring relationship, and I know that he was in fact much worse than this before he began seeing you for counselling. So perhaps you're doing better than you can give yourself credit for. I sense too that you want to say 'What about me? I need some support too when I'm coping with so many things in my work and life!'

Marjorie: (laughing) Yeah, dead right! Yes. I know this isn't the place to go into it, but sometimes lately I do wonder how much I can take. I'm giving and listening all the time, and not getting much back for it. Maybe I expect Anthony to reward me for my efforts.

Supervisor: I think we've worked together long enough for me to know that you're unlikely to fall into the trap of wanting the client to gratify you. But at the moment things are tough, and it's coming out here. It's OK with me if you need to talk a little about that and how it's affecting your work.

The supervisor does not make the mistake of slipping into or encouraging personal therapy to take place, but equally he does not ignore or postpone giving attention to Marjorie's personal needs. Having supervised her for some time, he realizes that her work is of a high standard and that in discussing Anthony, the client, she is discounting much of the valuable work she has done previously. His intention here is to offer just enough time to her to see if she can shake off some of the feeling of being stuck. Her laughter may be an indication that she needs to feel that her stress is recognized; a little validation and catharsis may go a long way. In another case, it may be that the counsellor has reached the limits of her capacity to help clients and should seek personal therapy.

Experienced supervisors will be able to discriminate, and to help supervisees discriminate, between transient difficulties and disillusionment, and more serious impasses. They should feel secure enough and be flexible enough, in our view, to offer support and permission at times of exceptional need. They should also encourage supervisees not to judge themselves for experiencing negative reactions and not to conceal them, but to acknowledge and learn from them.

Key point

Allow supervisees to disclose any feelings and reactions to clients, client groups and their work as a whole, and decide together within your contractual framework what is the most helpful way to explore and deal with these issues.

---

16 Offer constructive and clear feedback

Friedlander et al. define feedback in this context as 'a statement, with an explicit or implicit evaluation component that refers to attitudes, ideas, emotions or behaviours of the trainee or to aspects of the trainee–client relationship or the trainee–supervisor relationship' (1989: 151). We would add that of course feedback also occurs between experienced counsellors and their supervisors. We also agree with Bernard and Goodyear (1992) that it is possible to regard all communication – implicit and explicit, verbal and non-verbal – between counsellor and client, and counsellor and supervisor, as feedback of sorts. However, as a supervisor, you need to consider exactly what you want to get across to supervisees in each session in a manner that will enhance their work. Rioch (1980) points out that many supervisors offer clever interpretations of their own to explain supervisees' clients to them, but that these 'brilliant performances' frequently leave supervisees no better equipped to help their clients.

Whatever model of counselling and supervision you espouse, and whatever supervisory foci you predominantly utilize, it is worthwhile considering exactly what you hope to achieve and whether your feedback is as clear, constructive and helpful as it might be. What are the factors which impede clear feedback? Some examples are the following:

1 Assumptions about the counsellor, his or her existing knowledge and professional vocabulary, may lead the supervisor either to talk down or to talk 'over the counsellor's head'.
2 Differences between the supervisee's and supervisor's culture, class and other significant social variables, may lead to misunderstandings, as the discipline of sociolinguistics demonstrates.
3 The different preferred modalities of the counsellor and supervisor may lead to a mismatch in expression and understanding (for example, when the supervisor employs a lot of visual metaphors to make points, and the supervisee is much more of a 'doer' than someone who understands imagery) (Lazarus, 1989).
4 The supervisor's emotional reaction to the counsellor may lead the supervisor to convey conflicting messages or overwhelming criticism (for example, discrepancies between overt 'strokes' and non-verbal disapproval, or angry authoritarian outbursts).
5 The supervisor may offer non-specific feedback in global terms ('I think you're doing really well' or 'You've got a lot of improvements to make') which do not identify precise areas for consideration.
6 The supervisor may, in inspirational or excited mode, throw out a great many ideas and suggestions, leaving the supervisee feeling bombarded by too much diverse feedback at once.

This list could be extended but is intended to show that there is ample scope for miscommunication. The authority which supervisees often invest in supervisors may influence them to blame themselves for not understanding or remembering exactly what their supervisors have said or meant when they leave the session. Stop to think whether you have conveyed clear and mutually understood messages and cultivate the practice of summarizing your points, or asking your supervisee to help summarize them, before the end of each session. To clarify, we give some examples of good and bad feedback.

Supervisee: I feel really good about this client because she's far less depressed than she was and she's begun to take risks in her life.

Supervisor: That's just what worries me. Risk-taking is not invariably a sign of mental health and I have the feeling that you're being bought off. This flight into health is not to be taken at face value. What is she really saying to you?

Supervisee: Sorry?

Supervisor: What is her behaviour trying to alert you to?

Supervisee: Well, I didn't think there was anything negative or complicated in it . . .

Supervisor: See if you can identify the game that's being played next time.

Supervisee: The game? Er . . . yes, yes, I will.

In this example, the supervisor is rejecting the counsellor's understanding of events as too shallow, yet fails to explain the reasoning for this. The supervisor omits to check on what the risks actually were and assumes they are some form of 'acting-out' and avoidance. The term 'flight into health' is used without checking on its meaningfulness to the counsellor. The supervisor continues the volley of somewhat authoritarian interpretations and challenges until the supervisee becomes confused, probably feels deskilled and demoralized and pretends to agree and conform. The feedback would have been improved if the supervisor had been more tentative, had used plainer language, explained her own views and presented them as alternative rather than correct views.
Here is a different example:

Supervisor: Thank you for your very full case notes. I think I have a clear picture of the client and of what you're trying to do. If I may, I'd like to point out one or two areas in which I am still a little unclear.

Supervisee: Yes, of course. I'd appreciate hearing it.

Supervisor: You said that your client became tearful when you mentioned that your own mother had died. I'm not sure exactly what your disclosure meant to her and what you had intended by it. I'm aware that you use rather a lot of self-disclosure and I would like to understand why you did so here.

Supervisee: Yes. Well, I sensed that the client's mother's death was very important and yet he couldn't allow himself to stay with it. I wanted to give him permission, as it were, to feel its importance and to understand that it might be healthy to talk about it. Are you saying that I self-disclose too often?

Supervisor: No, I'm not. I simply wanted to understand your thinking here, and now I do, and that seems very useful as an intervention. That's fine. I'd also like to tell you that I think you've worked well with this client, by which I mean you've shown an excellent grasp of his needs and you've followed and enabled him in what he's had to do.

This supervisor has been much clearer. Her feedback involved some challenge and request for the supervisee to account for her particular intervention, yet without attack. It was feedback clearly tied to specific interactions, yet also related to broader positive feedback. There is little or no jargon and the supervisor shows a readiness to account for her own reasoning and to adapt if necessary.

Supervisor feedback does not always have to be positive, but should always be constructive. In other words, even when it is necessary for the supervisor to convey doubt, criticism or approbation, this can and preferably should be done constructively, so that the supervisee learns from it. Feedback needs to be specific, contextualized, jargon-free, mutually understood and useful. It is possible that a supervisor might offer feedback in a heated, passionate, spontaneous or irritated manner, and this kind of emotional response may well, on occasion, speak volumes to the supervisee. However well motivated by 'congruence' such feedback may be, it is not useful unless it is understood in the sense you intended and if it is isolated from concrete work with clients. If you do find yourself giving feedback passionately, check afterwards that its meaning has been clear!

Key point

Consider the quality of communication between yourself and supervisees and the many ways in which its clarity can be diminished, and strive to improve the constructiveness of your feedback in each session.

17 Avoid an overly cosy and possibly collusive supervisory relationship

Often there is a collegial atmosphere in supervision, or at least in those supervision relationships in which there is no assessment requirement. Counsellors who have graduated from training, at whatever level, may experience anxiety about their competency and about particular cases, but are likely to be more relaxed about evaluation. Supervisors and counsellors alike may sometimes feel that they are in the same boat, struggling to help clients, and that a friendly and facilitative climate is suitable for this task. Some supervisors certainly regard supervision as less taxing than counselling itself and may be tempted to approach it in a more casual manner. It is generally true, perhaps, that supervision is less emotionally laden than counselling, since client problems are discussed at second hand and supervisors are specifically prohibited from converting supervision into counselling. Counsellors who are paying for their own supervision will probably choose a supervisor with whom they feel comfortable; likewise, counsellors in peer supervision choose compatible colleagues. These factors taken together can have the effect of creating a rather safe, bland, unchallenging climate.

A better scenario than this is not necessarily an abrasive, confrontational or persecutory supervisory relationship, however! Certain therapeutic approaches which espouse minimal input from the counsellor and tight control of the therapeutic frame, for example, may replicate a rather austere climate in supervision. We have spoken with counsellors who have described their supervision as 'persecutory', meaning that the supervisor seemed intent on scrutinizing, interrogating, challenging and rarely supporting the counsellor. According to Strozier et al. (1993) the supervisee may be helped primarily by supportive, exploratory, restructuring and relationship factors. The supervisee in this (single case) research, appreciated being encouraged to work at understanding his client, but 'challenge' was not perceived as the most helpful factor. This corroborates our own experience as supervisors that supervisees are best helped by a purposeful supervisory agenda which includes high levels of support and exploration, with challenges emerging from that context.

The 'challenging but not overwhelming' principle (Dryden, 1991a) applies as much to supervision as to counselling. This concept argues that too low or too high a level of arousal is to be avoided in favour of levels of arousal most helpful to each supervisee. We have observed that clients are often not helped either by models of counselling which border on the aggressive or the passive (Dryden and Feltham, 1994b). A certain degree of dissonance in the supervisory relationship is likely to lend leverage to both supervisor and supervisee. Contrast this with the scenario in which both parties are inclined to great and invariable warmth towards each other and a mutual commitment to the same theoretical outlook. This combination may include the possibility of congruent challenges between supervisee and supervisor but contains a danger of fostering too much agreement or too narrow an approach (see Section 19). A commitment to genuineness, in the person-centred tradition, would in fact imply that both supervisor and supervisee would constantly monitor this quality in their relationship and both accept responsibility for articulating any diminution in its presence.

Perhaps one of the key indicators of a supervisory relationship edging towards the overly-cosy is the length of time it goes on. There are no agreed limits to how long any single supervisory dyad should ideally last, although some commentators suggest two years as a guideline figure. Certainly if you have been supervising anyone for many years, it is worth considering whether this arrangement is as beneficial for the growth of the counsellor and his or her effectiveness with clients as it might be. This is not a matter of change for the sake of it, but a recognition of the likely limits of how helpful protracted supervision relationships are.

One way of focusing on this issue is to examine supervisor countertransference. How do you feel about your supervisee? What is your overriding thought, feeling or image about your supervisee? What fleeting feelings and images do you have in sessions that relate specifically to your supervisees? What moments or hours of vague discomfort do you experience? Are you aware of liking your supervisee immensely and feeling thoroughly in tune with him or her? Are there any instances of erotic countertransference? In short, what is there between you and your supervisees which may not be strictly related to client work? However, we are emphatically not suggesting that liking your supervisees is wrong or unhelpful! Rather, we suggest that an audit of gains and losses of continuing supervision be considered from time to time. How much danger is there of blind spots creeping in between you? These are the kinds of questions you may wish to take to your own supervisor or consultant.

If you do suspect that there is something too intimate or too easy about your relationship, how will you broach this with the supervisee? Let us examine an instance of this:

Supervisor: I realize that we've been seeing each other for three-and-a-half years now. I really enjoy working with you, I must say. I have begun to wonder lately, though, whether we might look at your future, and ask whether continuing with me is for the best, or whether a change might be beneficial.

Supervisee: Well, it hadn't really occurred to me. Like you, I enjoy our sessions and I get a lot from them. It suits me to come here.

Supervisor: I don't think there is any great problem between us at all. What I'm suggesting is that your professional development might be helped by a change of supervisor, to someone perhaps with a different orientation, perhaps a man rather than a woman, for example.

Supervisee: Well, you may have a point. I need to think about it.

In this example, there is some reluctance for each of the people concerned to confront the possibility of ending the relationship, yet the supervisor has felt a need to raise the subject. The supervisor begins to discuss reasons for a possible change, as well as some of the possible ingredients of a change (perhaps a fresh theoretical approach, or a different gender match). Sometimes this kind of conversation may appear to come 'out of the blue', but if you have been following the practice of scheduling review sessions, this is something that might always, or often, be on the agenda: 'How long have we been meeting together and is this arrangement still fruitful for your needs and those of your clients?'

Key point

Look out for any tendency for your relationship with supervisees to become too flat, comfortable, protracted and unchallenging and seek to remedy this by discussion or corrective measures.

IV Using the
Developmental
Opportunities of
Supervision

18 Focus on and challenge supervisees' grasp of theory and translation of theory into practice

Counselling is a purposeful activity which is grounded in a body (or bodies) of knowledge. All BAC recognized training courses are required to demonstrate that they have a core theoretical model within them (see Section 5). This requirement underlines the importance of counselling psychology and other conceptual areas to the development and underpinning of the work of counsellors. Occasionally a trainee or supervisee will protest, when asked to account for his or her work, 'I just used my intuition' or, 'It just felt right.' Now, intuition and feelings are of course central components in counselling practice, but they cannot be used to justify the whole of one's work as a counsellor. Intuition and feeling can be thought through, explained and examined and, in our view, need to be investigated in supervision. Even where feelings, hunches and intuition are essential parts of certain orientations, as they are in the humanistic approaches, supervisors have the task of encouraging (and in training settings of requiring) supervisees to account for their affective methods. Indeed Goldberg (1992) commends 'emotion as a guide to purpose', and Back (1973) notes the crucial role of 'theory input' in even the most experientially-oriented encounter groups.

The need to focus on and challenge supervisees' grasp of theory probably relates more to trainees and counsellors in the early stages of their development. Both the groups of therapists represented in Dryden and Spurling (1989) and those by Goldberg (1992) expressed a certain dissatisfaction with their original theoretical training. It seems that clinical and life experience frequently compels practitioners to adjust their views. But does this imply that the training of counsellors can afford to omit altogether the theoretical component? We think not. The requirement that counsellors be 'reflective practitioners' (BAC, 1990) means that they must be exposed to the plurality of theories of human functioning and dysfunctioning, models of treatment, theories of lifespan development and psychiatric and ethical issues, in order that they can test their own 'naive' views. There is an immense danger in counselling of practitioners closing themselves off to new or challenging ideas and relying exclusively on their own views, opinions and subjective preferences. We must make it clear that we are not advocating anti-subjectivity and promoting a false 'objectivity'. Rather, we suggest that an optimally effective counsellor will refer constantly to personal *and* to external sources of information and inspiration. Indeed, the trend towards integration in counselling and psychotherapy suggests that theory, skills and practice are best viewed as intertwined (Ivey et al., 1987).

It is extremely unlikely that any counsellor will practise without some understanding of the concepts of the unconscious, transference, countertransference, empathy, distorted thinking, boundaries, developmental stages, self-sabotage, and so on. It may be confusing that there are so many different schools of counselling and that the language of counselling is expanding all the time (Feltham and Dryden, 1993). Nevertheless, there are central concepts, differently expressed in each of the schools, with which counsellors must be familiar. Every model of counselling has its unique explanation for counsellor intentionality and client change, for example. None says, 'Well, we just do whatever comes to mind and if it doesn't work, we try something else.' Psycho-dynamic counselling is based on various concepts of inner conflict; the counsellor's tasks being to bring these conflicts to the client's awareness, to make timely interpretations and to promote sufficient working through. Cognitive therapists understand clients' disturbances in terms of distorted thinking patterns, working towards their identification and replacement with more rational and productive thinking. Client changes within counselling can be accounted for in these terms. Supervisors in these examples need to be sure that their supervisees understand theory not only in their essays and discussions but in practice.

It is important to state that theory is not promoted and supervised for its own sake and we are not advocating dogmatic adherence to clinical theories. We are advocating that practitioners utilize theory flexibly as a guiding principle in their work. Even highly structured theories such as transactional analysis recognize the need for flexibility. But how does the supervision of theory and its application look in practice? Here is an example:

Supervisor: So, according to your understanding, the purposeful removal of the client's obvious defences (her smoking, sexual acting-out and passive-aggressive behaviour) would lead to her being closer to her deepest pain, is that it?

Supervisee: Yes. She agreed to try. She stopped smoking and sleeping around and she began to be more assertive. In theory this should have put her in touch with that time in her life before she resorted to avoiding tactics, to a time when she was still open to feeling pain.

Supervisor: You say 'in theory'. That seems to imply that in practice it didn't work out. How do you account for that?

Supervisee: Having thought it over and listened to the tape, I've realized that removing all her main defences in that way probably plunged her into an *overload* of pain, which she couldn't feel, so she had to compensate by resorting to desperate intellectual defences. In fact she became very talkative, wanting to understand and explain everything.

Supervisor: Which can have its place, but for her it was counter-productive? So this tells you, to refer to the theory again, that defences need to be dismantled gradually and sequentially.

This example shows the supervisor referring to both theory and practice, helping the supervisee to understand why, in this case, the theory first appeared to prove accurate but then appeared unhelpful. The supervisee was encouraged to 'account for' this apparent theoretical failure and realized that there was a valid theoretical view which helped to inform a better understanding of the client's 'pain threshold'. Rarely are theories monolithic, black and white structures; often one's understanding of particular cases can be enriched by returning to the intricacies of theory.

Another way in which theory can be useful is on those occasions when counsellors lose sight of their beliefs and guiding principles, for example at times of stress, disillusionment or near-burnout, by encouraging supervisees in this condition to return to their ideological roots, to recall their original excitement and stimulation in studying seminal texts and grappling with transformational new concepts (see Kopp, 1977). Sometimes a high ongoing caseload of clients can have the effect of draining the counsellor's emotional and intellectual capacities, leaving him or her operating only on a pragmatic basis. A radical reconsideration of theoretical fundamentals can sometimes restore purpose and clear thinking to counsellors in this position. So consider both the macro and the micro aspects of theory and its applications in your supervision.

Key point

Use the theoretical aspects of counselling to stimulate, challenge and guide supervisees, reminding them that counselling is both an affective and a cognitive activity and that a balance between these and other modalities is optimal.

---

19 Challenge supervisees on the possible limitations of their approach with particular clients

When you and your supervisee share the same theoretical and practical orientation, you may be quite unlikely to look for and challenge the limitations of your orientation. You may challenge supervisees on their application of the orientation with particular clients, but how much allowance do you make for the possibility that in certain cases clients need an approach other than yours? Alternatively, if you are an eclectic supervisor and your supervisee is aligned with a single orientation, to what extent will you attempt to stay within his or her theoretical frame, as opposed to using your eclecticism to challenge the supervisee? In this Section we will presuppose that you are, at least to some extent, more eclectic, integrative or broadly-based in your approach than your supervisee. (A discussion of the differences between eclectic and integrative approaches is given in Dryden and Feltham, 1994a.)

One of the most common examples of this issue is the counsellor whose approach is mainly relationship-based (person-centred or psychodynamic), encountering a client whose problem is anxiety attacks. The counsellor may conceptualize the problem as stemming from early separation anxieties or as related to the client's mistrust of his or her own organismic valuing process, for example. Such counsellors may regard this problem as amenable to a lengthy working-through process or to restoration of positive self-regard through these approaches. Yet clinical wisdom and a certain amount of research (see for example, Frances et al., 1985; Hallam,

1992) suggest that certain approaches may be more effective treatments for particular client problems than other approaches. In other words, there is at least good reason to stop and think 'Are there any indications that my (or my supervisee's) approach has important limitations in this case?' We believe that it is ethically imperative that supervisors and counsellors ask themselves such questions, rather than stubbornly maintaining that their approach can always deal with every conceivable client problem. Davenport (1992) goes even further and suggests that, in an American context, failure to raise such questions may be not only ethically unsound but legally perilous. The BAC *Code of Ethics and Practice for Counsellors* states that 'counsellors should monitor actively the limitations of their own competence'. Obviously individual counsellors' competence is constrained by the limitations of their training orientation and, logically, they and their supervisors should monitor these boundaries in practice.

What other examples might there be of such limitations? Imagine that a client has come to a community counselling service which, because of lack of funds, is forced to offer strictly time-limited counselling. Some basic training has been given in cognitive-behavioural interventions. The client, Glenda, discloses in the fourth session (out of a possible maximum of ten sessions) that she has been sexually abused throughout her teenage years. The counsellor, anxious to work effectively within the agency's constraints, believes she can continue working with the client. The client has little money and the only NHS facility for long-term psychotherapy has a waiting list of 18 months. As the supervisor, what will your comment be in this situation? We think it would probably be best that the counsellor offers what she can, while informing her client that longer-term counselling may well be necessary, and possibly helping her client to seek and secure such help.

Roger is 39, he is married with two children, has a successful job and is not in distress. Yet he feels a certain lack of meaning or direction in his life. He visits a local counsellor, recommended by a friend. The counsellor works psychodynamically and begins gently eliciting thoughts, feelings, memories and dreams, as well as pointing out instances of transference in the counselling relationship. In supervision, the counsellor reports that this client seems very resistant to all interpretations. As an eclectic supervisor, your judgement is that the client is experiencing a mid-life existential crisis which is not psychopathological in nature, and that he needs help to explore his current dilemmas and life values. How will you put this to the supervisee? We might challenge the supervisee to expand his views in this case and to consider a referral if he is unwilling to, or if he believes he lacks suitable skills.

Anne is a 29-year-old woman living in a hostel who tells her counsellor that she has never had a close emotional or sexual relationship with a man. In supervision, the counsellor tells the supervisor that she wonders about the client's sexual orientation: the reason for her lack (avoidance) of relationships with men may be that she has unconscious or suppressed lesbian needs. The supervisor, having heard other details of the client's life, suspects that the client has had a very deprived early life, in a rather inadequate family which discouraged friendships and largely kept to itself. The supervisor wonders whether the best strategy might be to offer social skills training. How is this discrepant view to be broached? We would suggest here that both views be aired in supervision and a thorough consideration be given to their merits before suggesting to the supervisee that she might explore these hypotheses sensitively but directly with her client.

All these examples present cases in which the counsellor has in mind either tentative or definite directions for the client, and the supervisor believes an alternative approach may be better. We do not wish to suggest that these cases are of an 'either–or' nature, since clients often benefit from a mixture of interventions or a 'technically eclectic' approach (Lazarus, 1989). Indeed, it is often necessary to offer, in early sessions, a kind of trial therapy, in order to ascertain whether clients can benefit from a particular approach to their problems. But in these cases there are dilemmas, particularly where the counsellor may be fiercely wedded to a chosen orientation. The most difficult scenario for the supervisor would be that in which he or she strongly believed that the approach offered by the counsellor was completely unsuitable, yet the counsellor was unwilling to compromise or unable to adapt. In practice this scenario is probably rare because counsellors tend to select supervisors compatible with their own orientation, but it may materialize.

Supervision from a single theoretical position may have certain problems but there are also the problems of developmental needs and limitations. In the case of a trainee who is in the early stages of learning about and applying a core theoretical model, for example, is it realistic or ethical to challenge the trainee on the limitations of this approach? In such a scenario, the requirement to offer supervision that is congruent with the supervisee's orientation (see Section 5) may sometimes be at odds with particular clients' needs. As the supervisor, your primary task is to help and protect the client, not to nurture and unconditionally feed the developmental needs of the counsellor. As Vandecreek and Harrar (1988) point out, trainee counsellors are obliged, with the help of supervisors, not to provide substandard care, and the supervisor is obliged to ensure that clients' needs are held as paramount. Faced with this dilemma, will you attempt to stretch your supervisee's abilities, caution him or her that this approach is too limited, or insist that the supervisee refers the client on to a practitioner with a more apposite orientation? Our view is that it is important to raise and discuss all such issues with supervisees, however inexperienced they are, in the interests of their clients, but that such 'confrontations' should always be effected with due sensitivity.

Key point

Consider whether certain clients would benefit more from counselling approaches which are beyond the supervisee's orientation and what steps you would take to ensure that clients receive optimal help.

---

20 Be aware of research findings and professional developments and encourage supervisees to acquaint themselves with these when it is helpful to do so

Many counsellors dislike, disown and avoid the area of counselling research altogether. We have discussed this subject elsewhere (Dryden and Feltham, 1994b) and pointed out our reasons for believing that familiarity with pertinent research is likely to improve counsellors' functioning. Imagine that you had trained as a counsellor 20 or 30 years ago and that you still adhered largely to your training orientation in its original form. Imagine that you had read no research or reports on professional development during that time. You might be completely oblivious to the advent of certain innovative approaches to counselling (for example, cognitive therapy, solution-focused brief therapy, neurolinguistic programming) which could hold promise for some of your clients. This extreme scenario is an unlikely one, but it may suggest that the more familiar with counselling research and professional developments you are generally, the better equipped you will be both as a counsellor and supervisor. There is probably a greater ethical and professional onus on supervisors and trainers to keep up to date with research and other professional developments than there is on those counsellors who bear no supervisory or training responsibilities.

Davenport (1992), in her critique of client-centred supervision, suggests that an adherence to one theoretical orientation which amounts to dismissal of research evidence and its clinical indications may be unethical and even legally perilous (in the USA). She specifically cites the example of a seriously depressed client for whom cognitive-behavioural therapy would be indicated and suggests that failure to consider or recommend this option may amount to negligence. Ask yourself as a supervisor, then, 'Should I be (and indeed am I?) familiar with research concerning treatment of choice?' Do you believe that your chosen approach to counselling holds the keys to client success in all cases? Do you think your approach has any limitations, for example with suicidal, psychotic, addicted or borderline clients? What is your understanding of how your approach effects change in depressed, anxious or anorexic clients? Whether you simply ask colleagues for their views, or consult case studies or rigorous research studies, you are at least demonstrating an awareness that these questions are important. As a supervisor, you may be faced with questions from supervisees about the wisdom of relying on person-centred counselling with clients suffering from post-traumatic stress disorder, for example. Alternatively, you may wonder whether your supervisee's valiant efforts to counsel a person with obsessive-compulsive problems has any prospect of success. How will you know? We think it crucial that you either familiarize yourself with research on these issues or that you have access to specialists, or at the very least that you urge your supervisees to consult appropriate sources or specialists themselves.

Barkham (1990) summarizes many of the issues concerning research in counselling and psychotherapy. Some of the questions addressed in his writing focus on the effectiveness of counselling in the short and long term; the differential effectiveness of various forms of counselling; the effectiveness of different counsellors; the optimal length of counselling; and cost effectiveness. Supervisors should be aware of some of the fundamental findings (and counterclaims) of researchers. Perhaps the most fundamental question in counselling research is: does it work? This has been debated now for several decades and there are heated 'yes' and 'no' responses. Many counsellors decide to regard such questions as merely 'academic', since they 'know' that counselling works because they have witnessed its effectiveness. Clients rarely ask for research 'proof', but we have known one or two clients who have asked 'What does the research say about whether panic attacks can be alleviated by counselling?', for example. Counsellors and supervisors may resort to reflecting the question back ('You'd like me to tell you what the research says . . .') but we believe this to be evasive. Clients have some right to want to know and get a fair answer. 'I don't know what the research says', may be honest, but not necessarily helpful. The same applies to supervisees. You may choose to tell them that you do not know what the research indicates on certain matters, but your honest ignorance may begin to tax their faith in you at some point!

We do not wish to avoid objections to research. It is sometimes said that counselling research concentrates on discrete problems so removed from real human life that it has no real value to counsellors in their actual practice. The comment is made that for every piece of research claiming to demonstrate something, there is another piece contradicting it. One of the most puzzling kinds of research is that which suggests that there is little or no difference in outcome from one theoretical orientation to another (Smith et al., 1980). Such research has led some to believe that it is the therapeutic relationship, regardless of theoretical rationale or supposed techniques, which effects change. Others, more cynically perhaps, argue that people usually get better (or worse) regardless of whether they receive counselling or not. Does research necessarily lead to dismally inconclusive inferences? Our belief is that research helps us to guide our counselling practice. In other words, it is often indicative of certain trends. The weight of evidence against any one orientation being decisively more effective than any other has led to fruitful considerations about eclectic and integrative ways of working, for example. If it is not primarily the theoretical orientation which influences change, perhaps there is something significant about client individuality and psychological type (Bayne, 1993). Engagement with research, even to a small degree, can stimulate the practice of counsellors and supervisors. You may also wish to consult the growing research on supervision itself (see Holloway, 1992). For a discussion on methods of counselling research, see Wampold and Poulin (1992).

In addition to research, you are likely to add to your supervisory skills and knowledge by keeping abreast of developments in counselling generally. New techniques are constantly being created and experimented with, and although some of these may prove to be ineffective or transient, some will no doubt improve the repertoire of counsellors and supervisors. Increasing concern for accountability in counselling and psychotherapy is leading gradually towards a professionalized structure. One of the signs of this is BAC counsellor accreditation, as well as course and supervisor recognition. We are aware that beginning counsellors are very concerned about accreditation and often require guidance in preparing to apply for their own accreditation. Supervisors cannot afford to be ignorant of such developments. Trends towards National Vocational Qualifications (NVQs), concern for effective brief counselling in certain settings, and the search for integrative models are all significant areas of development with which supervisors are advised to be acquainted.

Key point

Familiarize yourself with the reasons for consulting research studies, know the central issues in research and be prepared for supervisees' implicit and explicit questions bearing on research and professional developments generally.

---

21 Suggest that supervisees undertake further training, reading and personal development work as necessary

Charged with having an oversight of the work of counsellors, you will almost inevitably come to realize supervisees' individual strengths, deficits and needs. As a practitioner who is usually more experienced than your supervisees, you probably have a more in-depth familiarity with the whole field of counselling, its specialities, developing trends, significant research, reputable training courses and so on. Hopefully, you will not be the only professional colleague to whom your supervisees can turn, but in some cases you may be. We have known counsellors working within organizations who have been professionally isolated (for example, a lone counsellor working in an advice centre) and counsellors working in private practice who have very few professional contacts. All counsellors are expected to engage in some form of periodic retraining, but some can afford to partake of very few such opportunities. With all these factors in mind, and remembering the distinctions drawn between supervision and training (see Section 3), how will you decide whether and when to intervene to suggest to supervisees that they explore certain avenues of further development? Here are some illustrative examples.

Rosie has a diploma in counselling and works part-time in a mental health organization. She encounters a wide variety of client problems and feels ill-equipped to deal with some of them. She is under some pressure to undertake time-limited counselling but acknowledges that her training paid little attention to the efficient use of time. She is a dedicated worker who makes the most of resources. As her supervisor, you realize that she might well benefit from certain reading material and possibly from certain workshops. You might specifically ask her if she would like to spend some time within supervision looking at such options. A planned session might be put aside in which to discuss them. You might even wish to bring into the session some books which you want to suggest or lend, and course or workshop brochures. Some supervisors might object that this is more of a trainer or consultant role, or that the supervisee should find these things out for herself. We see no harm in offering this information ourselves in the supervisor role and advising supervisees on what may be suitable courses and books. A reading of Budman et al. (1992), for example, might help to sharpen awareness of the factors involved in time-limited work. Workshops on brief therapy and assessment methods might help Rosie to enhance her skills within the work setting.

Brian has completed a certain amount of counsellor training and is about to undertake further training. He has had some personal therapy in the past. In supervision sessions he often raises the question of his own suitability for and commitment to counselling. From listening to his tapes and to his accounts of his cases generally, you believe that he has some excellent qualities which suit him for work as a counsellor. Specifically, he asks you for your view on whether some further training in either transactional analysis or cognitive-analytic therapy would be better for him.

Since your impression is that his main problems are self-doubt and perfectionism, you might suggest to him that he finds a counsellor or therapist with whom to explore this further. You may, alternatively, know of a group which would be appropriate for him. It is even conceivable that he would benefit from some psychological assessment and careers counselling. An important point here is that if such self-doubts recur frequently, then some form of non-supervisory assistance is indicated, and it is part of a supervisor's responsibility to raise this. As we have stated earlier, we are against the kind of curt dismissal of supervisees' concerns which is heard in the sentence, 'That's not appropriate material for supervision, you must take it to personal therapy.'

There are many variations on these themes. A supervisee may commend herself for participation in a Gestalt therapy group that you are familiar with, because she is concerned in supervision about her discomfort with strong feelings. Another supervisee may want to know about multimodal therapy because he has heard that it may be more systematically helpful than the orientation in which he trained. Yet another supervisee may seek your views on psychoanalytic training because she seems to be constantly encountering deep, transferential material that she feels unable to cope with. In each case, you are faced with the decision about your supervisory role and the best use of supervision time. It is because the supervisor has, we believe, a consultant function, or even a guidance role, that we consider it wise to include this element in your supervision. Ultimately, you are helping to protect clients by ensuring that counsellors themselves receive the help, direction or encouragement they need.

In review sessions, it is worth considering a formal evaluation, along with your supervisees, of areas where a need for improvement is indicated. By referring to Appendix 3, you may be able to help supervisees identify such areas. In discussion together, you may identify recurring weaknesses in working with catharsis, for example, or with behaviours and cognitions. If these deficits are serious enough or recur often, or if supervisees express a particular wish to build on their expertise, you may work with them to identify a helpful action plan. The supervisee who wishes to improve understanding and skilful use of cognitive-behavioural counselling methods might benefit from a little pertinent reading, or a short course, or more extensive training. The supervisee who demonstrates a recurrent problem of defensiveness within his or her work, however, may need to be directed towards personal therapy or other forms of personal development work. In some cases, supervisees may benefit from undertaking personal development work by bibliotherapy, for example by studying Burns (1980) on cognitive therapy or by using the Jungian-inspired method of journal-keeping commended by Progoff (1975). It is not antithetical to the spirit of supervision, we believe, to negotiate homework assignments with supervisees who seek help in improving their counselling in specific areas. See Dryden and Feltham (1992) on the use of homework assignments.

Key point

Allow time and consideration to be given to supervisees' developmental needs in relation to further training, reading or varieties of personal development work.

---

22 Share your own clinical and developmental experiences with supervisees when it is helpful to do so

Counsellors are generally schooled in the assumption that they should self-disclose to their clients very sparingly, if at all. They are also alert to the temptation to do clients' work for them. These attitudes are sometimes understandably carried forward into super- vision, so that many supervisees do not expect their supervisors ever to disclose any personal or professional experiences of their own, nor to indicate to them what they should do in particular cases. There is much to be said for the kind of supervisee-centred supervision, in which the supervisor may regard the main task to be facilitating the counsellor's self-understanding and self- determined clinical progress. There is also a clear rationale for the 'opaque supervisor' who allows supervisees to project into the supervision situation and to work through their own obstacles in order to achieve greater insight into their clients.

We believe, however, that a valuable formative aspect of supervision is supplied by the supervisor's willingness to share openly personal experiences and views. Let us clarify immediately what we do *not* mean by this. 'I remember when I was a young counsellor and I hadn't a clue what was happening from one session to another' is the kind of ostensible openness and humility that is too sweeping and may actually undermine the supervisee's confidence in the supervisor and in the counselling profession. 'I had a case just like yours years ago and today I still get letters from her telling me that counselling changed her life' is the sort of statement likely to undermine the supervisee by suggesting, possibly, that brilliant interventions are made by brilliant practitioners which may not be replicated by less experienced counsellors. It may also come across as embarrassingly boastful. 'In my experience there is no cure for this kind of anorexic client' – this statement, full of pessimism and authoritarianism, leaves the supervisee with nowhere to go. 'Just between you and me, like you, I've once or twice crossed ethical boundaries – it's only human' – the supervisee hearing this 'confession' is apparently being 'forgiven' but is invited to collude in the supervisor's implication that ethical transgressions are, after all, not to be taken seriously. These examples demonstrate that thoughtless self-disclosures, or even well-intentioned but ambiguous disclosures, are to be avoided.

The following two examples are to act as the basis of a discussion of what may be considered helpful supervisor self-disclosures. In the first, a male supervisor, Trevor, listens to his male supervisee Ben, telling him that one of his female clients came to their last session wearing extremely revealing clothes. This seemed to be uncharacteristic of the client, and the counsellor was 'thrown' by it. He found himself slyly looking at his client's legs in the session. Ben also speculated that his client may have been sexually abused as a child. He was fully aware of his own, real sexual feelings towards his client, but also alert to the 'informational value' of his feelings (Searles, 1955). Ben was aware, too, of his feminist colleagues' perspectives on the vulnerability of women clients with male counsellors. Trevor sensed, however, that although Ben seemed to be in touch with all these elements, he was labouring under some suspicion that he might be 'at fault'. Trevor decided to disclose to Ben that he had often felt strong sexual feelings towards women clients, that he regarded these as natural, and that by accepting them in himself (without, of course, acting on or being significantly distracted by them) and examining them for clinical meaning, he believed he had come to understand many of his clients better. After sharing this with Ben, he initiated yet further discussion of Ben's views generally and on the client in particular.

In the second example, Moira discusses her client with her supervisor, Alice. The client is a woman who has been experiencing anxiety attacks for some months and has been seeing Moira during most of that time, apparently without significant progress. Moira explains that she has spent a considerable time helping her client to explore family dynamics and present circumstances, she has often focused on the client–counsellor relationship, and she has encouraged the client to undertake certain behavioural assignments. 'Honestly', she declares, 'I just feel like I'm not getting anywhere with her, and I keep talking about her here, and I've even told her that I feel stuck, but all to no avail.' Alice has indeed heard the details of this case frequently and has even been party to helping Moira decide on strategies. She has heard herself say to Moira, 'You seem to think that *you* are getting nowhere and that *you* are stuck, and perhaps you've got yourself into that position by thinking you've got to rescue the client.' She has heard herself say all sorts of clever and sensitive things to Moira. Now, she chooses to say, 'Well, to be honest, I think we all encounter clients who can't, or don't want to change, or for whom we are not the best counsellors. I know I have. Like you, I've struggled with some clients with whom there's been very little progress.'

In the first example, where ethical and countertransference issues are under consideration, the supervisor wishes to reassure the counsellor that he is not alone in his dilemma, that he is not a sex fiend, and that there is probably great positive value in examining his feelings in relation to the client. The second example concerns the counsellor's experience of a continuing impasse, in relation to which she is beginning to berate herself for not coming up with effective interventions. Here again, the supervisor decides that it is timely to self-disclose and to suggest that impasses are sometimes just that – impassable – based on her own experience. (A subtle myth in the counselling profession is that if only you just keep going, keep having faith in the process, or hit on the right 'door to therapy', one day the client – every client – will change.) In both these cases the supervisor decides to offer normalizing statements which say, 'I have been here too and what you are experiencing is genuinely difficult.' This is, of course, quite the opposite of the withholding, rather persecutory style that certain supervisors may practise (see Section 28).

Supervisor self-disclosure is not intended to pre-empt what the counsellor can discover for him- or herself. In the above two cases, the supervisors might in different circumstances decide, depending on the timing, not to disclose their own experiences and views. They would certainly not make their own disclosures important in themselves, nor devote time to reminiscing about them. Supervisors should obviously guard against breaching confidentiality in such cases and should be mindful of their purpose in choosing to self-disclose, as well as anticipating the effect their disclosures may have on the supervisory relationship. There may be occasions on which some disclosures of a more personal nature may or may not be helpful. For example, a statement by a supervisor such as, 'I'm actually going through a divorce myself, so I imagine that what your client is telling you about her sense of being judged by her family is no exaggeration', might shock the counsellor into understanding the client better, or it might lead the counsellor to lose respect for the supervisor. There can be no formulae for supervisor self-disclosure but there is justification for its timely use.

Key point

Consider the possible variety of supervisor self-disclosures, when they may or may not benefit the supervisee, and share your own professional or relevant experiences judiciously.

V

Highlighting Supervisees' Strengths and Weaknesses

23 Help supervisees to identify their best cases, best interventions and predominant strengths

Beginning counsellors who are working with their first one or two clients sometimes experience self-doubt if there appears to be little evidence of progress. Often, this is because there *is* little discernible progress, and this lack of progress may simply be a reflection of a particular sample of difficult clients. The particular danger of working with only one client is that the client may become the problematic 'only child' of the counsellor, receiving almost too much attention and becoming the counsellor's sole source of evidence of counselling ability. As counsellors themselves progress to work with a larger number of clients and a wider cross-section of clients, they are able to compare the counselling they are doing from one case to another. Inevitably, counselling with some clients proceeds far better (more smoothly, rapidly, dramatically or successfully) than with others. Sometimes this may be fortuitous (Arnold Lazarus, in Dryden (1991c) suggests that about 40 per cent of all clients improve regardless of the kind of counselling offered them) but sometimes It indicates significant factors in the counsellor's work.

We have found it very beneficial, almost from the beginning of supervision, to encourage supervisees to review and compare their own cases. In which ways do all their cases resemble each other, if at all? In which ways are some cases experienced as difficult and 'stuck', while others are experienced as enjoyable and rewarding? What are the specific features in each case from which counsellors can learn more about the counselling process and about their own professional development? Even when a counsellor is seeing only two clients, it is possible and fruitful to ask the counsellor to identify with some precision the factors contributing to feelings of frustration or progress in the work with each client. This sort of focus encourages a variety of action research: if supervisees can begin to reflect on why they look forward to certain clients but dread others, for example, then they can use these reflections to challenge themselves in future sessions.

So you might ask a supervisee, 'Of your two cases, with which one do you think you're working more effectively?' When one is identified, proceed to ask, 'What are you doing with this one, or what is the nature of this relationship, which enables you to work more effectively?' Detailed scrutiny of counsellor intentions can then proceed. When your supervisee has seen a number of clients over a period of time, you might ask, 'Which two or three clients stand out in your mind as representative of your best work?' or 'With which two or three clients did you experience most satisfaction?' One of the purposes of such questions is to help supervisees to discriminate between different kinds of client, different kinds of client–counsellor match (or mismatch) and different counsellor responses. Another purpose is to switch the focus in supervision from inconclusive work-in-progress to work completed. In looking back over past cases, especially their 'best cases', counsellors can be encouraged to learn from success and to celebrate it.

Since a great deal of counselling (and therefore supervision) concentrates on the pathological and the problematic, a useful sense of balance is restored by looking at reasonably clear examples of success and satisfaction. This might be called 'success-focused supervision' in parallel with solution-focused brief therapy (De Shazer, 1985). Focus on success helps supervisees to value their own work and to consider what part they played in the progress of clients who experienced successful outcomes, instead of attributing such success merely to chance. When you are guiding supervisees towards examination of their successes, take care not to ask for instances of 'dramatic cure'. Mearns (1990) suggests that success is often better understood in terms of process rather than product. In other words, clients' reports that they 'feel much freer to express anger and sadness', or 'more readily own disappointment instead of hiding it', for example, indicate typical successes. Mearns cautions against the fairy tale version of success and you would be wise, too, not to help supervisees demoralize themselves by searching for their own fairy-tale examples of success with clients.

By encouraging supervisees to refer back to notes and tape-recordings, it is possible to identify the kinds of typically successful interventions they have made. Use the Hill and O'Grady (1985) list of therapist intentions (Appendix 3) to focus on what supervisees are doing particularly well. It may be that a supervisee has a special ability 'to instil hope', 'to identify maladaptive behaviours', or 'to resolve problems in the therapeutic relationship'. You and the supervisee may agree on a 'short list' of the supervisee's particularly effective interventions. There may be identifiable trends (the supervisee may often challenge clients, for instance) or there may be a number of outstanding therapeutic moments (the supervisee may have voiced certain inspired hunches or promoted the use of dreamwork or imagery). Allow the supervisees to experience these as their own, to learn about them and to 'chalk them up' as successes.

Similarly, but more broadly, we suggest that supervisees are encouraged to identify their overall strengths. These may take the form of 'I think I'm very warm and easy to be with', or 'I'm not afraid to take chances and challenge the client', or 'I seem to have a natural ability to visualize keenly the narrative clients describe to me'. As often as not, strengths have their reverse side (the warm counsellor may be weak on challenge, the challenging counsellor may lack warmth) but here it is important to suspend such questions and to help supervisees derive satisfaction and morale from accepting that they have strengths. Indeed, one of the pressing questions for beginning supervisees is often 'Am I doing all right?' Attention to the micro skills of counselling or to the details of clients' cases, often leaves supervisees wondering whether they are broadly performing adequately. It is vital, in our view, not to forget to have supervisees periodically recall their strengths and successes.

If you engage in long-term supervision with counsellors, you will have the opportunity to raise and discuss with them what you both consider to be your most memorable sessions and most fruitful interactions. You may be able to celebrate together the progress of certain clients about whom you have had extensive case discussions. You may wish to instigate, at review sessions or informally, discussions about the particular strengths of your working alliance. Comparisons of the supervisor's with the supervisee's strengths are sometimes useful. You may, with some justification, point out to a supervisee that you admire the extent of her ability to disclose her own feelings to clients congruently. 'It took me much longer than you to learn to trust my own feelings and disclosures', might be a supervisor disclosure which could accurately honour a supervisee's strengths in this area. It is of course important that as a supervisor you are not defensive about any weaknesses that you may have as a practitioner and that you are capable of offering generous feedback to supervisees when required.

Key point

Suggest to supervisees that they reflect on the satisfaction of the work they do and the successes they have with different clients, in order to learn about their own strengths and to generate morale.

---

24   Listen carefully for any recurring lacunae relating to supervisees' skills and conceptualizations

Students and beginning counsellors are often highly selective about what they take from their training and what they put into practice. For example, many trainees avidly demonstrate their ability to track accurately and empathically their clients' statements, yet omit altogether, or largely, some of the skills relating to genuineness, such as confrontation and immediacy. Sometimes counsellors have conditioned themselves so well not to ask questions that they unwittingly spend all their time reflecting and failing to gather some of the essential information they need. The 'pervasive anxiety' of the beginner often explains why certain skills are over-used or under-used: in their anxiety, counsellors may feel bombarded by tutors' expectations and take time to internalize skills to the point where they are used as 'second nature'. Sometimes, however, even in very experienced counsellors, a habit may develop of never confronting clients, never asking questions, or always relying on identifying feelings and attempting to produce catharsis, for example. (Heron (1990) refers to this latter practice as the 'cathartic treadmill'.) In other words, for various reasons, many, if not most, counsellors are vulnerable to overdeveloping certain skills and neglecting others.

Similarly, counsellors may allow themselves to think rather narrowly about their clients. Depending upon their training orientation, counsellors may be induced to be alert for instances of transference, irrational thinking, confluence, games, and so on.

More broadly, they may listen exclusively for signs of psycho-pathology instead of being aware of the healthy, coping behaviours of their clients. Any rigid, single-theory orientation is likely to foster narrow conceptualization of client cases. The opposite scenario may be the kind of chaotic eclecticism which encourages counsellors to think of all possible variables in each case but which offers them no way of gauging when to place particular value on the most helpful concepts for each client. In this latter scenario, a counsellor may well be able to generate dozens of ideas about what may be wrong with the client, and how they may be helped, but may then suffer from clinical indecisiveness.

The supervisor who listens carefully for supervisees' recurring lacunae does so in order to be able to offer constructive feedback. The purpose of such an exercise is not to wrong-foot the super-visee, and it is not based on the assumption that every counsellor should master every possible counselling skill, technique, strategy and conceptualization. Our focus here is on the ways in which counsellors inadvertently emphasize certain skills and conceptual tools, and overlook others. This is a complex subject because it is built into the very fabric of the therapeutic enterprise where each school of counselling emphasizes certain phenomena and plays down others. The ability to tune into, focus on and work in depth with strong feelings is highly valued and developed within certain humanistic approaches (for example, primal therapy, psychodrama, Gestalt therapy and experiential psychotherapy) but is de-emphasized in others (for example in the cognitive-behavioural therapies generally). The training does not exist, as far as we know, which equips counsellors with the entire range of possible skills and interventions.

Most basic counsellor training expects that trainees will have an understanding of and a degree of competency in addressing clients' feelings. Trainees are taught to reflect the content of clients' statements but also to be sensitive to and to reflect, when appropriate, clients' expressions of significant feelings. Counsellors who have difficulty experiencing and valuing their own emotional life, however, frequently develop the same lacunae in relation to clients. We have listened to tape-recordings of counselling sessions in which the counsellors have very accurately understood and conveyed their understanding to clients of the factual content. At the same time they have altogether omitted to reflect or comment on their clients' sad, faltering voices, heavy-hearted silences and other signs of emotional turmoil. If, as a supervisor, you do not listen to supervisees' tapes, then you will not know from such evidence how they respond or fail to respond to affective cues.

You may still, however, note from the way they discuss their clients that the accent is always on the factual and rarely on emotional undercurrents.

The opposite case might occur where a counsellor is highly attuned to feelings and frequently homes in on them, at the same time omitting to attend to clients' actual behaviour between sessions, their counterproductive beliefs, and so on. At its most dangerous, the effect of highlighting strong feelings and ignoring clients' ability to cope has resulted in client deterioration and even suicide (Masson, 1988). There are many variations on these themes. If you emphasize counsellors' skills in the use of time-limited counselling you may risk overlooking the needs of fragile or severely damaged clients. If you emphasize the skills and values relating to long-term transference-based therapy, you may risk clients becoming unhealthily dependent and passive. Because we believe strongly that each client deserves the best possible available service, we think this implies that supervisors need to maintain a somewhat flexible outlook, if not an attitude of responsible eclecticism. As a supervisor, your ethical commitment is to help counsellors address the actual needs of clients. When clients need forms of therapeutic assistance which are not being delivered, either because the counsellor lacks the requisite skills or the organizations involved do not provide certain kinds of training or support, then you are bound to discuss this with supervisees.

How might you broach this subject? Consider the following dialogue:

Supervisor: Sonia, I've heard a few of your tapes as well as many of your own case discussions and, as you know, I think you are very skilful in the way you help your clients express their concerns and unravel their histories. What I'm not so sure about is where it all goes from there. Your clients Charles and Denise, for example, who I know you've been seeing for almost a year, seem to me to be stuck.

Counsellor: I . . . I hadn't thought of it in that way. I don't think I'd say they were stuck. They have a lot to work through, both of them.

Supervisor: In some sense that may be true, yes. But as I recall, it's been difficult for you to interrupt either of them, to help them summarize their stories and to inject some structure into the counselling. We've talked about this before and I think you acknowledged that you find it hard to change this kind of meandering, almost aimless kind of counselling.

Counsellor: Yes, we did talk about that. It is something I have trouble with, yes. I hadn't realized it was still there, and noticeable. When things get to this stage with clients, I just don't feel I can try and change anything.

Supervisor: Maybe we can go over again what we discussed before, as well as listening to some recent tapes, and see exactly what's happening. If you agree, we can look at what may be missing on your part, and perhaps role-play some different interventions. How does that sound?

In this case, the supervisor has had to introduce her concerns without invitation (except in so far as the original contract may have included the responsibility of the supervisor to make known any areas of concern she had). This is not immediately welcomed by the supervisee, who initially feels defensive. The supervisor links her current remarks with earlier comments and gains the supervisee's acknowledgement that there is indeed a recurring tendency to allow certain counselling relationships to lose most of their focus. The supervisee appears to be on the edge of becoming demoralized, when the supervisor sensitively suggests some positive actions in a non-judgemental manner.

In Section 10 we discussed specific interventions and you may find it useful to consider, when you supervise, ways of gauging exactly which interventions your supervisees use most and which kinds of case conceptualizations they most commonly refer to. By using Hill and O'Grady's (1985) list of therapist intentions (see Appendix 3) you can begin to determine the gaps in supervisees' practice. Don't do this as a kind of secret detective activity, but enlist your supervisees' support and understanding in doing it. Explain that all practitioners, however senior, have a tendency to overdevelop certain skills and to rely too much on certain concepts, and that an occasional 'audit' of these imbalances can usefully identify the resulting lacunae. When this exercise is successful, the supervisee is able to say, for example, 'I realize that I rarely challenge my clients, that I rarely comment on my clients' strengths, and I want to examine these gaps and improve them.'

Key point

Attune yourself to the skills, strategies and conceptualizations that your supervisees emphasize and those, accordingly, which they neglect, and help them to address these positively.

---

25   Identify and explicitly raise for discussion any obvious errors and avoidances in supervisees' work

Counsellor errors may be considered broadly in two categories: those which do no significant damage and those which do. Occasional errors may include lapses of attention, failure to remember important parts of clients' stories, poor timing of interventions, giving unsolicited advice, rescuing the client, missing important cues, allowing a session to run over time, and so on. These are probably common errors and may sometimes be perpetrated by experienced as well as beginning counsellors. Provided that they are not repeated frequently, that counsellors are not unaware of them, and are actually able to learn from them, they need not be of grave concern. Indeed, in some cases, there is evidence that clients find occasional instances of counsellor fallibility reassuring.

The kinds of counselling errors with which we are more concerned are those outlined in the growing literature on therapeutic failures and iatrogenic counselling (Strupp et al., 1977; Robertiello and Schoenewolf, 1987; Striano, 1988; Howe, 1989). We list here some of the main groups of errors.

1 Pushing clients too hard or aggressively in the belief that they need to uncover and break down their defences. Certain approaches to counselling and psychotherapy espouse vigorous challenging of clients' defences and certain individual counsellors impulsively or omnipotently practise such approaches. The results can be that clients may become confused, emotionally overloaded and in extreme cases psychotic and even suicidal.

2 Omnipotently interpreting clients' material in the belief that as the counsellor one knows better than the client what is going on inside them. While most counsellor training stresses the importance of accurate empathy and an understanding of the client's frame of reference, this does not prevent some

counsellors from developing a dangerous sense of their own power and incisiveness. Clients may be bewildered, undermined and grossly abused by such an attitude.

3 Inadequately assessing clients' suitability or readiness for counselling. Many people are referred for counselling without wishing it for themselves or without understanding what it involves. Some counsellors enthusiastically take on all referrals without due caution. Clients may present with anxiety or stress symptoms, for example, who actually have undetected organic or neurological problems. In such cases, suitable treatment may be delayed and, in extreme cases, clients receive unnecessary and even counterproductive counselling.

4 Failing to gain clients' informed consent to counselling. Many counsellors make the assumption that clients should not need to know anything about counselling in advance of actually receiving it. The implicit rationale that counselling is some sort of mysterious process, which cannot or should not be explained, is held, we believe, by far too many counsellors. An ethical therapeutic alliance consists of a working rapport, an agreement on the goals of counselling and on the methods to be used.

There are many more examples that could be given besides these but this list at least provides us with a starting point for the debate. As a supervisor, how are you to gauge whether supervisees' behaviour as counsellors falls into any of these categories of error? Overt and obvious examples of such errors are one thing, but as we argue elsewhere, you have no way of ensuring that supervisees present every aspect of their work and, without access to tape-recordings, you can have little direct evidence of what they do in counselling sessions. Often counsellor errors may be inferred. For example, if a supervisee's clients seem to become confused, or deteriorate, too frequently, or if the counsellor has an unusually high drop-out rate, then you may begin to ask questions. But if the counsellor conceals this drop-out rate, or describes the cases in a way that is favourable to his or her own self-image of a competent counsellor (when several of the clients are deteriorating, perhaps), then you may simply not suspect or learn of it. Also, in the worst scenario, you and your supervisee may share certain blind spots. If you both subscribe to a forcefully cathartic approach, for example, you may interpret clients' regressive experiences as signs of progress or temporary resistance, when in fact the client may be deteriorating. This scenario brings home the need for supervisors to maintain their own supervision arrangements and to consider receiving supervision from practitioners whose orientation may be usefully different from their own.

When, however, you are able to identify errors, how will you raise this subject? Here is an example:

Supervisor: You've talked about your client getting 'spaced out' and apparently resisting your work together by often becoming confused. You seem to have referred quite a bit to the client's crying, her stopping herself from crying, and your efforts to get her to 'stay with the feelings'. Can you tell me what you actually say to her, and what your therapeutic rationale is?

Supervisee: Well, she often looks moist-eyed, but brushes her tears aside. Her voice is often low, as if she's refusing to let her real feelings out. I sometimes say, 'Let yourself cry, don't hide it', and 'Say that louder'. I believe she keeps herself sick by keeping it all inside and I want to encourage her progressively to trust her own feelings.

Supervisor: I understand, yes. From what you say, though, she seems to have difficulty in expressing feelings, and it may be that she's expressing all she can at any one time. How do you know when to push her? How can you be sure this is for her own good?

Supervisee: Intuition, I guess.

Supervisor: Well, perhaps. But my intuition, on hearing your description of her and her 'spaced out' behaviour, is that she may be being pushed harder than she can handle. I know you believe strongly in this cathartic approach, but let's consider whether it's right, at this time, for this client.

The supervisor knows how the counsellor works but asks her to account for her approach with this particular client. She is not afraid to express her own reservations about this piece of work. She does not denigrate either the counsellor or her approach, but expresses specific doubts about the client in question in relation to the approach. It would probably not be helpful to declare, 'You are making a serious mistake.' In the same way that counsellors can never really know what is right for their clients, so supervisors rarely, if ever, know exactly whether supervisees' interventions are erroneous. In this case, however, the supervisor feels strongly enough about it that she is prepared to pursue it. For the supervisee to learn from this kind of supervisory intervention, challenge and exploration are necessary.

Egan (1990) refers to counsellors' avoidance of necessary challenging as the 'Mum' effect. In other words, at those very times when clients need to be confronted with something that is at variance with their own views or claims, some counsellors persistently make the error of avoiding challenge. Counsellors may be afraid of upsetting the client, afraid that the client may turn upon them, afraid that they have 'got it wrong', and so on. Unwillingness to interrupt the client, to offer risky feedback and to make a stand, characterizes some beginning counsellors but may arise for any counsellor in relation to particular clients. A counsellor who is unconsciously reminded by the client of an angry father, for example, may unconsciously seek to placate the client, instead of challenging helpfully. It is often easy to appear to be silently understanding when in fact one has not understood the client. Avoidance of negative statements and feelings is far from uncommon among counsellors (Regan and Hill, 1992).

By its very nature, avoidance is often harder to detect than overt error. The supervisee may claim, for example, that 'I have quite often confronted the client about his drinking.' It may only be by listening to a tape-recording that the supervisor would realize that the 'often' was really seldom, and that the confrontation was delivered in an unchallenging tone of voice. Attention to parallel process may sometimes yield clues to what is being avoided between client and counsellor, but you are advised to seek other means of determining what may really be happening within sessions. When a supervisee says that a particular client always arrives late in spite of being challenged about it, consider using a role-play. The supervisee takes the part of the client and you take the part of a researcher or, perhaps, the client's partner or friend. As the researcher or friend, introduce the idea that it is easy to mess the counsellor about, and let your supervisee (in the client role) explore how true this is and what may be involved in it. Encourage the supervisee to learn what may be going on from the client's perspective.

Key point

Consider the kinds and degrees of errors and avoidances in your supervisees' counselling, initiate constructive exploration of instances of these and help supervisees to learn from them.

---

26   Assist supervisees in identifying both helpful and unhelpful countertransference issues

As counsellors, the feelings, thoughts, sensations and images we have about our clients, which we learn to become conscious of, hold the potential to sabotage or enhance our effectiveness. Whether we work psychodynamically or not, we are well-advised to pay constant attention to the messages we receive indirectly from and about our clients. We have elsewhere discussed some of the many emotional and unconsciously communicated nuances in the counselling relationship (Dryden and Feltham, 1994a). Casement (1985) is a leading exponent of the concept of self-supervision, based on the counsellor's learning to understand clients' often unconscious and coded messages. Counsellors who have developed a heightened sense of the variety of subtle impacts clients have on them may be able to monitor their own countertransference rapidly and accurately both within and between counselling sessions. Even so, supervisors can usually lend a profitable, objective perspective to counsellors' self-supervision.

When a counsellor reports that 'I really don't like this client,' or 'I always feel very sleepy in my sessions with Ron', these may appear to be limitations of the counsellor but they warrant closer analysis. It is also often a possibility that a client is conveying an unconscious message to the counsellor. In this case, the female counsellor may be unconsciously 'made to feel' dislike for the client by his subtle negative behaviour. The counsellor may experience herself as being unable or unwilling to help the client. She may find it hard within sessions to muster sufficient wakefulness and interest to apply herself to the client's concerns. What might the client be 'saying' indirectly? Certain clients have powerful feelings stemming from very early childhood which apparently cannot be conveyed directly and verbally. When they cannot verbalize such feelings, they may well 'get under the skin' of the counsellor in powerful and unconscious ways. It is when counsellors have initially unaccountable feelings about clients that important countertransference issues are often being flagged up. Supervisors can help their supervisees to remain open to the idea that potentially useful messages are being conveyed in these feelings. When countertransference is ignored, or incorrectly attributed to the supervisee's 'pathology', valuable opportunities are missed and the supervisee may feel blamed instead of helped.

Robertiello and Schoenewolf (1987) give an interesting list of common errors made by counsellors and therapists, which involve some failure to identify instances of countertransference stemming from the counsellor. They discuss the case of a therapist who, after a period of pronounced negative transference from a particular client, became the object of the client's intense erotic transference. The therapist, feeling threatened by homosexual expressions because he had not dealt with such aspects of his own sexuality, quickly encouraged the client to terminate therapy rather than deal with his own countertransference. In this case, the work was clearly of a psychoanalytic nature. Whatever the theoretical orientation of the counsellor, however, counselling effectiveness is likely to be diminished by counsellors who remain unaware of countertransference limitations or who stubbornly refuse to entertain the possibility that defensive countertransference may be at work. A supervisor, on hearing of this therapist's sudden eagerness to terminate with such a client, would need to be alerted to countertransference in operation and to help the supervisee to explore it. 'It seems that very quickly after your client has changed from being very hostile to being very positive and even erotic towards you, you feel compelled to dispatch him: that seems like something worth exploring' is the kind of supervisory statement that might prevent a hasty termination and lead to a fruitful new area of work.

It is apparent that counsellors choose to discuss what they believe is 'problematic', 'interesting', 'straightforward', and so on, in the supervisory context. In group supervision when counsellors are asked to bid for limited time for their cases, for example, often someone will have an 'urgent' case, another will have 'just a general issue' and others will say they have 'nothing really, no problems'. It then becomes apparent that one counsellor's perception of urgency, for example, is another's idea of a straightforward case. Supervisors would do well to note the ways in which supervisees present, or avoid presenting, their clients. We believe that in training contexts it is essential for all students to discuss their cases regularly. Even among more experienced counsellors, however, it is important that supervisors ask themselves why certain supervisees rarely seem to have any urgent, interesting or noteworthy cases to discuss. Equally, you may note that some counsellors always seem to have burning issues. We suggest that such phenomena are not accidental, but may indicate significant, concealed countertransference issues.

In individual supervision, too, look out for the manner in which supervisees sometimes discuss particular clients endlessly, yet pass over other clients as if they are of no interest. It is worthwhile suggesting to your supervisees sometimes that they undertake to discuss their omitted or underrepresented clients at great length and to omit or temporarily put aside their favourite or problematic cases. This kind of 'shake-up' may well force supervisees to reconsider exactly why they devote inordinate amounts of supervision time to certain clients, yet little or none to others. For example, on being asked to talk about a client who she often referred to as 'straightforward' and who, she declared, she 'really liked', one supervisee initially had great difficulty explaining this case to her supervisor. As she struggled to articulate her work with the client, it was evident that it had become a collusively intimate relationship from which the counsellor was deriving comfort and fascination, but the client was gaining little in relation to her objective in coming for counselling. In another case, which the counsellor had described as 'just a straightforward bereavement case', it emerged that the counsellor, unable to deal with the emotions stirred up in himself by the client's loss, had unconsciously 'flattened' the counselling, turning it into a rather routine, supportive chat.

Let us now take a slightly different perspective on countertransference. Suppose that you and your supervisee work within an agency which offers time-limited counselling that is predominantly cognitive-behavioural in orientation. As the supervisor, you are talking over with the counsellor how he has been helping his client to overcome his social anxiety. The counsellor, however, laments the slow progress his client is making. Turning your attention to the counsellor's own self-statements in relation to this case, you and he discover that he actually, to some extent, despises the client's timidity because, when he himself was younger, he had much the same problem and he overcame it vigorously. The counsellor was then telling himself that his client should be able to change more rapidly and, more subtly, that if he failed to change quickly, then this would reflect badly on his (the counsellor's) own view of himself. Although the term 'countertransference' is of psychoanalytic origin and has many meanings, not all counsellors think in these terms. What is important is that all supervisors have some concept similar to it, listen for traces of its various manifestations, helpful and unhelpful, and energetically unearth and utilize its power.

Key point

Help supervisees, individually or in groups, to identify and explore their thoughts and feelings about all clients in order to reduce unhelpful countertransference and to harness productive countertransference.

VI Protecting the Client and the Counsellor

27 Be alert to counsellors taking on too many clients or exceptionally difficult clients, and intervene accordingly

Trainees enter counsellor training with different professional experiences behind them. Some are very experienced counsellors already, for example, who decide to retrain or to engage in refresher training. In such cases, these counsellors may already be working in private practice and may have an established caseload of clients. As far as we know, there are no published guidelines as to what are considered to be acceptable maximum caseloads. In practice, beginning trainee counsellors often take on two or three clients and may spend a year seeing no more than three clients each week. We have heard of cases, however, of counsellors taking on a number of clients in different settings and even beginning private practice before being fully trained. We advocate a very gradual increase in client numbers and we would caution beginning counsellors not to exceed an average of about six client hours a week until they have gained a fair amount of experience. Over-eagerness to build a high caseload may betray a kind of indecent haste and an unwillingness to learn at a necessarily modest pace. (In some cases, of course, newly qualified counsellors are tempted to take on a large number of clients for economic reasons; this kind of pressure should be avoided, we believe, if at all possible.)

We have addressed the issue of the requisite ratio of hours of supervision to hours of client contact (Section 12). Obviously it is wise for the counsellor to increase the amount of supervision received commensurate with the number of clients being seen. However, there is a limit to the effectiveness of supervision, even when ample supervision is available. Counsellors are unlikely to practise at their most effective when they are seeing 30, 40 or 50 clients a week, even if they are receiving several hours of supervision each week. It is not possible to say exactly what the optimal number of clients is, because individual circumstances vary so much, and there are some gifted and energetic counsellors who have a large capacity. In general, it seems probable that after a certain point, counsellors may begin to feel drained, uncreative and even unable to distinguish accurately between each client's details. For the sake of the individual clients, it may be best if counsellors do not spend every hour of the day and evening seeing clients. But it is important for the well-being of counsellors, too, that they learn to recognize their own thresholds for effectiveness. As the supervisor, you may in some cases be the only professional colleague who is aware of how many clients a counsellor is seeing. We think it good practice to enquire from time to time just how many client hours counsellors are working each week, for example:

Supervisor: So, Jim, tell me, how many clients do you have at the moment?
Supervisee: Oh, er, about 12 or 15, I think, I'm not quite sure.
Supervisor: Well, I don't want to ask for a written record of every one of them, but I would find it useful to know how many you have, and therefore the kind of pressure you may be under.
Supervisee: Well, at the last count there were 16, but one has just finished and two or three come fortnightly. It might be an idea if I kept a running record and let you know from week to week, would it?
Supervisor: Yes, I'd find that helpful. It would help me to keep in mind your overall workload.

This brief dialogue identifies several issues. Here, the counsellor is not apparently threatened by the question and even seems to warm to the idea of producing an ongoing record. The supervisor explains the reason for wanting the information and a new piece of supervisory structuring takes place. The supervisor is, strictly speaking, responsible for monitoring that the counsellor is working ethically by checking that he is receiving an adequate ratio of supervision. If the counsellor had said, 'Well, I'm now seeing about 35 clients', the supervisor might immediately realize that the amount of supervision was inadequate to protect those clients' interests. The supervisor might also wonder why the counsellor apparently only ever talks about the same three or four clients every week!

Another variant of the counsellor biting off more than he or she can chew is found in the tendency to take on certain kinds of clients. As supervisors we have been aware of certain counsellors having an unhealthy tendency to attract more than their share of sexually abused, drug addicted, violent or suicidal clients, for example. (Of course, if counsellors work in drug rehabilitation centres and similar settings, then different considerations apply.)

When the counsellor is either 'putting out vibes' which attract certain difficult clients or is perceiving all clients as difficult, the supervisor needs to focus on and address this issue, for example:

Supervisor: Jane, I notice that among your eight or nine clients, at least six or seven seem to be seriously depressed. I don't know if it's just happened that way. I also wonder what cumulative effect this may have on you.

Supervisee: Yes, I know there are a lot, and I have wondered why I seem to get them all. My colleagues at the Centre don't seem to get so many seriously depressed clients, and yet they're apparently allocated randomly. I have wondered about it.

Supervisor: Well, from the way you've discussed your clients, I have the feeling that you work very responsibly and thoughtfully with them. At the same time, I have sometimes felt that you perhaps become very involved with them, and very 'fascinated' by their morbid preoccupations with death. Is there anything in that?

Supervisee: Are you saying that I'm identifying with them in an unhealthy way?

Supervisor: I'm not sure. I'm simply trying to explore this. It may be accidental that you seem to end up with more than your share of such clients, or it may not be. I think it's worth looking at, that's all.

In this discussion it is possible that the supervisee may begin to feel threatened. 'What is my supervisor thinking about me?' would not be an unnatural question to occur in the counsellor's mind. However, it is quite likely that such a counsellor would be unconsciously aware of the nature of his or her caseload and perhaps be waiting for the supervisor to ask this kind of question. If anything, it would seem unnatural to avoid asking such an obvious question. This supervisor directly but sensitively puts this question, inviting the supervisee to explore any meaning it may have.

Of course, it is sometimes the case that counsellors specialize in certain kinds of clients or client problems and do so consciously and competently. We are not suggesting that this should not happen. But it may happen unconsciously and pathologically and may have unfortunate repercussions for the counsellor, which is why it needs to be addressed. It is important to be vigilant with regard to supervisees' potential stress and burnout and to raise any suspicions that your supervisees may be courting burnout. In the extreme, when a counsellor persists in taking on too many clients or clients who are too taxing, then you may consider advising him or her to make reductions or changes, and even to *insist* if it appears that the counsellor is seriously depleted and cannot recognize this fact. Consult Dryden and Varma (1994) for examples of counsellor stress and their possible remedies. For an example of the peculiar stresses placed on counsellors working with seriously damaged clients, see the account by John and Marcia Davis given in Dryden (1992).

Key point

Watch for evidence that supervisees are taking on too many clients overall or too many difficult clients, raise this issue with them and deal with its implications as necessary.

---

28 Consider the range of possible abuses by counsellors and ensure supervisees are acquainted with these

Recently there has been a great deal of exposure of counsellors who seriously and blatantly abuse their position and undermine public confidence in counselling generally (Masson, 1988; Rutter, 1990; Russell, 1993). Sexual abuse within counselling is the main 'headline' aspect of abuse known to the public. However, there are many ways in which counsellors can, and unfortunately sometimes do, abuse their clients. Since supervisors are often the only people who are aware of counsellors' ongoing cases, the onus for monitoring for such abuse rests heavily upon them. Of course supervisors may not like the role of policing counsellors and anyway often have poor access to what counsellors actually do within their sessions. Perhaps supervisors find themselves somewhat constrained by needing and usually having to trust supervisees' own accounts of their work (certainly in the absence of audio- or video-recorded direct evidence) on the one hand, and themselves being to some extent accountable, if not 'vicariously liable' (Slovenko, 1980), for supervisees' work, on the other hand. Mearns (1991) describes the supervisor's experience of wrestling with these very issues.

Counsellors who abuse their position of power and trust with vulnerable clients are acting in a way that is humanly damaging and professionally unethical. Yet there is a spectrum of abuse from the unarguable cases of sexually unacceptable behaviour at one extreme to the debatable instances of minor transgressions at the other extreme. Arriving five minutes late for your client's session may be considered abusive by some practitioners, since it seriously 'violates the frame' of counselling (Smith, 1991), but it is hardly as damaging as sexually seducing the client. Frequent lateness on the part of the counsellor is obviously highly abusive. But there are many other examples of how clients may be subtly abused and it is part of the function of supervision to alert counsellors to these and to be vigilant in regard to possible instances of abuse. What are some of the possibilities for abuse?

First, there are overt, serious breaches of professional ethics. These include transgressing confidentiality and exploiting clients financially, sexually, emotionally or in other ways. This category of abuse or malpractice implies that the counsellor knowingly breaches ethical boundaries and jeopardizes the safety, privacy and well-being of the client. If you have explored the *Code of Ethics and Practice for Counsellors* with your supervisees, it is reasonably clear to them what is unacceptable in this group of behaviours. Nevertheless, you may need to explore subtle grey areas. What, for example, distinguishes therapeutic touch and hugging from titillation and the slippery slope towards sexual contact? (See Thorne (1987) for a vivid example of this dilemma.) What distinguishes the judgement that a client should be encouraged to have more frequent sessions (at greater cost) from subtle financial exploitation?

Second, there is the failure to respect clients' autonomy and personal and cultural values. The counsellor is always in a position of potential influence over the client. Ideally, any influence actually exerted is in the client's interests, but it is possible to persuade clients to embrace the counsellor's opinions and values and to overlook or demean the client's own values. There are myriad possibilities, for example, of failing to respect clients' ethnic sensibilities, the constraints of social contexts, the realities of oppression, preferences of sexual orientation and moral stance. Unfortunately it is possible for counsellors to exploit their position, wilfully or unwittingly, by swaying clients towards certain moral, religious, political or other ideological views. Issues such as abortion, sexual orientation and religious faith are prime examples. Varah (1985), for example, recognized that the Samaritans' clients are vulnerable to religious proselytizing and expressly forbade this practice. It is all too easy to believe that one respects another's culture, when in fact that respect may be experienced by the client as a rather patronizing attitude.

Third, there is the failure to adapt to the individual needs of clients. Too many counsellors and psychotherapists appear to be 'orientation-centred'. In other words, they put their attachment to certain theories and practices before the actual, highly individualistic needs of each client. The principle of informed consent is swept aside altogether and the client is expected to adapt to the counsellor's presuppositions about human development and preferred interventions. We have argued strongly elsewhere (Dryden and Feltham, 1994b) that clients' rights as adult consumers must be clarified and respected. Clients are not research subjects on whom we test out our precious theories, but people in some degree of pain or confusion requiring real help. As an example of what we consider bad practice, a woman suffering from panic attacks was referred to a psychotherapist in private practice who told her that she must attend sessions three times a week for at least two years (and must, additionally, pay fees even when she – the client – went on holiday). This may stem from a certain therapeutic tradition, but we believe in this instance at least that it was an abusive attempt to fit the client to the tradition and to the therapist's convenience. It would be equally abusive for a counsellor committed to 'quick-fix' techniques learned at a weekend workshop to take on and attempt to 'hurry up' a client who clearly needed caring, supportive, long-term counselling.

These are just some of the instances of possible abuse and we encourage you to consider your own list. Supervisors must be highly flexible and reflective in their own practice if they are to avoid perpetuating subtle abuses or failing to identify them when they occur. It is easy enough to discuss a Code of Ethics at the outset of a supervision relationship but it demands constant vigilance to monitor ethical practice. An intrinsic part of this vigilance is the monitoring of one's own ethical views as a supervisor. Do you think it is perfectly acceptable for a supervisee strongly to encourage a client who is on a low income to increase their sessions from once to twice a week? Can it be considered a form of abuse if the counsellor maintains a rigid, 'neutral' attitude when confronted by a bereaved client? The difficulty in these questions is that if you share a theoretical orientation with your supervisee which favours, or even insists on, frequent sessions and an 'abstinent' attitude, then you may be colluding in a kind of institutionalized abuse, in this case ignoring the client's financial constraints and human need for recognition of grief.

In parallel with these issues, consider the possible abuses of supervisees by supervisors, some of which we have mentioned earlier (see for example, Section 2). The power differential in supervision (particularly in one-to-one supervision provided by a senior colleague) can make for a dangerous assumption that the supervisor is always right. Park (1992) cites several cases of therapists who felt intimidated by their supervisors. Park suggests that supervisors often 'emphasize orthodoxy over spontaneity' and sometimes covertly discourage counsellors' candid disclosures about the realities of their work. Park cites one case of a supervisee who resorted to 'lies and concealment', so intimidated was she by her 'rigid, orthodox' supervisor. The worst case might be 'students with a narcissistic analyst whose views they are expected to absorb, and who have a dogmatic supervisor with whom they cannot discuss the issues' (Park, 1992: 68). Dogmatic supervision may be considered a form of abuse because it is likely to inhibit supervisees' development and creativity in the service of clients. Lazarus comments:

> I am put out by supervisors who give strong negative feedback to trainees. 'That was a mistake!' 'You should have waited for the patient to talk about her mother before you started addressing her sibling rivalry.' In such matters, how can anyone be so sure what the right thing is? (in Dryden, 1991b: 221).

Necessary ethical boundaries are one thing, but theoretical dogmatism is another.

Key point

Be aware of, and discuss with supervisees, the many possible forms of abuse in counselling and in supervision, and carefully monitor for instances of any abuse, however subtle.

---

29   Support the counsellor and encourage him or her to implement methods of self-nourishment and professional self-development

Strozier et al. (1993) reported that the supervisee in their case study valued highly the supportive interventions of the supervisor. They speculated that trainees may be more helped by 'concrete expressions of supervisor support', while more advanced counsellors may derive a more subtle sense of support from the supervisory relationship. Obviously most of us appreciate support in our work but, as this study shows, support is usually found most useful when it is accompanied by a judicious level of challenge. However, there are good reasons to suppose that supervision is most effective for most counsellors when it is grounded in a basically supportive relationship. We have heard of supervisors who announce ominously to new supervisees that they intend to be highly challenging. While this approach may stimulate some counsellors, we believe that on the whole a collaborative stance is likely to be more effective than an overly challenging one. Let us clarify what we mean here by support.

We do not equate support with 'propping up' or colluding with the counsellor. By support, we rather mean an attitude of acceptance and availability. At times support has the connotation of firm containment. It also alludes to a basic trust in the counsellor's work and a wish to see the counsellor flourish professionally and therefore gain in effectiveness with clients. It implies that the supervisor is capable of 'being there' for the supervisee in a usually non-reciprocal manner. Peer supervisors can of course support each other but in the supervisory relationship between a senior counselling practitioner and the supervisee there is implied a capacity for a special quality of nurturance. The supervisor is often in a position to offer supportive interventions in a way similar to the counsellor giving support to clients (Heron, 1990).

Whether you are supervising a beginning counsellor or someone who has lengthy experience, one of your key concerns should always be to protect the supervisee and hence his or her clients. It has been amply demonstrated in recent years that counselling and psychotherapy can and do exact a toll on practitioners (Guy, 1987; Goldberg, 1992; Dryden and Varma, 1994). The isolation of private practice, the strains of 'one-way intimacy', the effects on family life, organizational politics and other factors are commonly reported as stressful for counsellors, however much experience they have. As a supervisor, you are in a position to observe the effects of stress on your supervisees and to help them address these.

In Section 27 we discussed the problems arising from supervisees taking on too many or overly demanding clients. Here we wish to argue that counsellors are vulnerable to myriad subtle stresses and that these are better addressed than overlooked. So what will you do or say if you come to suspect, for example, that your supervisee appears exhausted, overworked and frequently breathless? The pressure on supervisors to avoid converting supervision into personal therapy can mean that you may avoid addressing these areas altogether. We consider this unwise. Many counsellors do excellent work, yet still get tired. Personal therapy is not, we believe, the universal panacea for all such ills. Counsellors may need to be reminded to take a holiday, for example, since private practice relies on actual client-contact hours and this can easily deter counsellors from taking time off. Counsellors also need balance in their lifestyle, so that they are not simply eating and breathing counselling and gaining no sustenance from relationships, leisure activities and life in its wider context. For example:

Supervisor: I notice how tired you've seemed the last few times we've met. Your work seems as professional as ever, yet perhaps it's taking a lot out of you.

Supervisee: Well, yes, I'm tired, I guess – things haven't been easy financially and I worry about that, and the kids are very demanding – but I hope I don't come across as distracted or stressed, do I?

Supervisor: No, you don't. You come across as if you need a break, but I realize that you can't afford a holiday as such. We talked at the beginning of our work about one of my responsibilities or tasks being to check out with you if your effectiveness ever seemed compromised, in line with the Code of Ethics. I see no current sign of that, but I think it might be worth discussing in a preventive sense.

Supervisee: Yes, I see what you mean. Yes, I'd welcome some time to discuss that. Is that OK with you?

This conversation depicts the scenario in which a counsellor is in danger of becoming over-stressed. When the subject is raised, she acknowledges a reality but is also a little wary. The supervisor effectively gives permission for this to be discussed non-judgementally. This would lead on to a constructive look at how the counsellor can find some way of getting some necessary rest within limited resources.

But what about the beginning counsellor who encounters serious doubts about competency? Michael has completed counsellor training and has begun to see three clients a week privately. He holds down a full-time job as a teacher besides this. He telephones his supervisor one evening to say that one of his very first clients has been admitted to hospital in an acute psychotic state. Michael is very upset but seems to be reassured that he had neither omitted nor committed any actions which would have caused or prevented this. At a subsequent supervision session, however, he begins to wonder aloud whether he is the right sort of person to become a counsellor. The supervisor asks if Michael would like to spend some time discussing this, since it is obviously of paramount importance. Although he says he feels guilty about 'taking up supervision time talking about myself', the supervisor believes that such discussion is a legitimate and indeed essential task at this stage. During the discussion, it emerges that Michael had endured taunts about his competency throughout his early life and these were being triggered by his thoughts and feelings about his client's psychotic episode. By the end of the session, he feels relieved and affirmed. The supervisor has helped him to unravel present and past distress and to resume his commitment to practising as a counsellor.

This is a form of nourishment within the session. The supervisor has judged that attention to his supervisee's emotional state temporarily needed to take precedence over case discussion. Where might such a scenario lead? In this case, for example, the supervisor had reason to believe that Michael was a highly competent counsellor in the making, one of whose main problems was his own exacting, if not perfectionistic standards. The supervisor suggested, accordingly, that Michael allowed himself a period of less intensive self-scrutiny in which he could feel free to find his own counselling style and to spend rather less time on note-taking, tape-recording, reading and reflecting. What the supervisor might have done, additionally, is to recommend that Michael considered his own self-rating and the irrational beliefs underlying them. Burns (1980) gives a useful account of perfectionism and how to reduce it, and books in this self-help format can be particularly recommended to supervisees who need to accept themselves rather than drive themselves to self-defeating stress levels and even burnout. As a supervisor, do not be afraid to suggest to your supervisees any such reading material and other stress management methods which will enhance their practice by encouraging them to look after their own needs. Self-development is not always a strenuous exercise but often an awareness of and changing attitude towards unhealthy habits and self-judgements.

Key point

Remember to be on the counsellor's side, supporting his or her efforts and at the same time being alert for signs of stress and self-doubt, for which you can make useful suggestions and interventions.

---

30 Maintain your own development as a supervisor, develop your own supervision skills in further training, and model professional commitment to supervisees

Many of us have, perhaps, fallen into the role of supervisor or had it 'thrust upon us' years ago. Since it is only in the last few years that any supervision training courses have been established in Britain, it is probable that many practising counsellor supervisors learned their skills 'on the job' rather than in formal training. Depending on the setting in which you work, you may be given opportunities to undertake such training, or you may be expected simply to accrue all required skills by sheer length of experience. Indeed, it is probably often the case that very experienced practitioners do have a great deal to offer supervisees on the basis of their own experience with a large number of clients and supervisees. However, it also happens that experience can foster complacency and blind spots. In this Section, then, we are concerned with your own ongoing development as a supervisor.

As well as passing through your own stages of development as a supervisor, you will inevitably have your own individualistic style, your own strengths and weaknesses. If you have worked in a great many different settings and seen a wide variety of clients and client groups, you probably have much to offer supervisees in terms of breadth of experience. When, for example, a counsellor asks you for your input on the difficulties involved in working with drug addiction, you can offer authentic and helpful comments if you have 'been there' professionally. If your experience has been largely in private practice with affluent clients and supervisees, however, you may have less experience of certain clients and you may have less to offer supervisees who encounter clients who are unemployed and facing multiple difficulties. It is recognized by the BAC that supervisors need to maintain their own direct practice with clients in order to stay in touch with the 'coal face' of counselling. We recommend that whenever possible, supervisors gain or maintain clinical experience in different settings and with different client groups. Between us, for example, we have worked in hospitals, voluntary organizations, residential centres, student counselling services, employee assistance programmes, private practice and many other settings. We value this kind of exposure because it brings us into touch with a wide range of clients from many walks of life.

As well as maintaining this 'hands on' experience with clients (and with supervisees in such settings) you are well advised to support your development as a supervisor by formal training. Now that there is an increasing number of supervisor training courses, do consider such training, even if you are an experienced supervisor. As well as encouraging you to reconsider the basics of supervision, such courses will probably challenge you to examine any deficits or underdeveloped areas in your own practice. Since counselling and supervision is very open to innovation, there is always likely to be a great deal to learn in supervision training about new models of counselling and supervision. (The recent interest in brief counselling and brief therapy, for example, may prove especially challenging and stimulating to supervisors who trained some years ago and have not had to confront the issues involved in time-limited work.) Also, training with others enables you to 'compare notes' and exchange stories of your experiences with supervisory colleagues. In the frequently isolated profession of counselling and supervision, such opportunities are to be welcomed.

One way of focusing your efforts to develop your supervisory skills is to consider applying for BAC supervisor recognition. Details of this process are included in Appendix 5. One of our colleagues who successfully completed this process told us that it was an extremely useful exercise in its own right and that it helped her to identify her strengths and renew her commitment. Accreditation and recognition procedures are often viewed as rather negative bureaucratic exercises, but their positive value is often in the fact that they validate the very skills that you do have. Exposing your supervisory style, skills and conceptualizations to the scrutiny of colleagues allows you to gain a fresh perspective on your work. Use Appendix 4 to rate your supervisor competencies.

There is a fine line to be drawn between the healthy pursuit of professionalism and the unhealthy obsession with counselling, supervision and training. In the latter case, when your life becomes totally dominated by the practice and discussion of counselling, then you may be shutting out the necessary dimensions of 'real life'. We do not advocate total immersion in the milieu of counselling and supervision. We believe, however, that within your professional sphere there is usually scope for some improvement. Obviously, counsellors learn much from their trainers and supervisors, often inadvertently as much as intentionally. The experienced counsellors writing on their professional development in Dryden and Spurling (1989) frequently cite supervisors as important formative influences. So, just as we are alert to parallel processes and other supervisee dynamics, we cannot ignore the influence that our own behaviour in supervision sessions has on supervisees.

It may not be your intention, for example, to encourage supervisees to emulate your counselling style and beliefs, yet it would be naive to suppose that supervisors do not have an impact, especially when they are highly experienced practitioners supervising less experienced counsellors. We ourselves would want to discourage any idealization on the part of supervisees, but at the same time we recognize that many supervisees probably covertly infer a great deal from our conscious and unconscious behaviour in supervision. One supervisee, for example, gradually made it apparent in supervision with one of us that she assumed that our experience was far greater than hers and that, accordingly, everything said by the supervisor must be the authoritative word on the subject and obviously far superior to any of her own insights! One of the key areas in which helpful modelling is required, then, is supervisor self-disclosure of limitations, doubt and sometimes plain ignorance. If your supervisee asks you, for example, for the benefit of your wisdom regarding clients with gambling problems, you may need to say, 'I've never actually worked with any such clients', or even 'I think I'd find it extremely difficult working with that kind of problem.'

Your own professional development as a supervisor may benefit from further training, intermittent personal therapy, research or other intellectual pursuits, teaching and workshop presentation, and so on. This should be tempered by attention to your personal life, relationships, adequate rest and recreation (Guy, 1987). Hopefully, this balanced concern for professionalism and personal health and integrity will demonstrate itself in the way you treat supervisees. It is sometimes said that supervision is a more relaxed, collegial activity than counselling itself. We believe there is some truth in this and that a great deal of the pleasure of supervising consists in the opportunity to learn about the counselling process with and from supervisees. Supervision is often more informal than counselling, perhaps involving greater self-disclosure and more humour, for example. It is simultaneously the 'serious business' of helping counsellors to maintain and hone their skills. Perhaps the most important aspect of supervisor development, then, is learning how to balance the professional and the personal, how to weave technique and relationship together. These are subjects to be taken to your own supervisor or consultant.

Key point

Assess what areas you need to continue to develop as a supervisor, balance your continuing professional education against your personal needs and be aware of the professional and human impression you make on supervisees.

Epilogue

It is our hope that supervisors and intending supervisors will be able to benefit from the points made in this book and that it will serve as a series of discussion points. It is likely that, depending on your particular theoretical orientation, on your level of development as a supervisor, and so on, you will find some aspects more useful or relevant than others. If your ambition is to become an 'all rounder' as a supervisor, able to respond to the needs of a wide variety of counsellors, then perhaps every section of the book may help you to remind yourself of the range of goals and tasks involved in supervision. Remember, however, that few supervisors can be all things to all supervisees.

With the increasing professionalization of counselling, we expect to see an increase in supervisor training courses and clearer statements about what levels of supervision are required by counsellors and by supervisors themselves. (The supervision of supervisors is an area we have not addressed substantially in the present book.) At the same time, we would add a caution about the pitfalls of professionalization. Not everyone agrees with the tendency for the development of counselling to be bureau-cratically packaged into the specialisms of training, practice and supervision. There are a number of counsellors who are con-cerned that an increase in professionalization entails a decrease in respect for counselling activities which do not conform with recent standards and requirements. There is also justifiable concern that acknowledgement of the place of common sense, love, humour and serendipity in counselling and supervision is not made.

We are aware that counselling and supervision can sometimes deteriorate into rather ritualistic activities. Since supervision is an activity that counsellors are *obliged* to engage in, there is a risk of it becoming, at times, a supervisory ritual offering minimal real learning. Because of this risk, we think it essential that supervisors and supervisees remain perpetually open to discussion and negotiation concerning the rationale and practice of supervision. One of our purposes in writing this book has in fact been to demystify supervision. Having said this, we welcome the publication of further texts and research on the subject and the establishment of excellent supervisor training courses. We also recommend that readers make themselves aware of the valuable ongoing work of the Standing Conference for the Advancement of Training and Supervision (SCATS).

Appendices

1 Presenting a client for supervision

Presenting a client for supervision – some frameworks for supervision and case study.

1. **Identification**
   1.1 A first name only. Gender. Age group/life stage.
   1.2 Your first impressions, physical appearance.

2. **Antecedents**
   2.1 Contact. How the client came to see you, e.g. self-referred.
   2.2 Context/location, e.g. agency, private practice, hospital clinic.
   2.3 Pre-contact information. What you knew about the client before you first met. How you used this information. Any existing relationship or previous contact with the client and possible implications.

3. **Presenting Problem and Contract**
   3.1 Summary of the client's presenting problem.
   3.2 Your initial assessment. Duration of problem. Precipitating factors (i.e. why the client came at this point). Current conflicts or issues.
   3.3 Contract. Frequency, length and number of sessions. Initial plan.

4. **Questions for Supervision**
   4.1 Key question(s) or issues you want to discuss in supervision.

5. **Focus on Content**
   5.1 Client's account of problem situation.
   (a) Work – significant activity, interests. How client spends his/her time and energy.
   (b) Relationships – significant people, family and friends.

From: I. Horton, (1993) 'Supervision', in R. Bayne and P. Nicolson (eds), *Counselling and Psychology for Health Professionals*. London: Chapman and Hall.

(c)   Identity – self-concept, feelings and attitudes about self.

Additional related or explanatory elements might include client's past/early experiences; strengths and resources; beliefs and values; hopes, fears and fantasies. Possible implications of cultural, economic, social, political and other systems.

5.2   Problem definition – (a) Construct a picture of the client's view of the present scenario; (b) What is the client's preferred scenario? What would client like to happen? How would the client like things to be?

5.3   Assessment and reformulation – how you account for and explain the presenting problem.
   (a)   Patterns/strands/themes/connections which emerge.
   (b)   In what way are these things important to explore? What theoretical concepts/models or explanatory frameworks for assessment? What hunches, new perspectives?
   (c)   What else, which has not been mentioned, might be important to explore? What silent hypotheses, blind spots? What underlying issues or past problems?

5.4   Counselling plan
   (a)   What direction or focus for future work? What possibilities, agenda?
   (b)   What criteria for change: theoretical frameworks and assumptions?
   (c)   Review and/or formulate plan(s).

6   Focus on Process

6.1   Strategies and interventions
   (a)   What strategies and interventions have you used?
   (b)   What were you trying to achieve?
   (c)   What was the effect on the client?
   (d)   Generate alternative options.

6.2   Relationship
   (a)   What was happening between you and the client? Describe relationship; reframe relationship; try a metaphor.
   (b)   What was happening within the client (transference)?
   (c)   What was happening within you (counter-transference)?
   (d)   What changes within the developing relationship over the period being discussed?
   (e)   Evaluate the 'working alliance'.

6.3 Evaluation
  (a) Review process.
  (b) Consider alternative tasks, strategies and ways of implementing counselling plan(s).

7. **Focus on Parallel Process**
  7.1 What was happening between you and the supervisor?
  7.2 Any parallels. What thoughts, feelings, experiences? Does what was going on in the supervisory relationship tell you anything about what may have been going on between you and the client?

8. **Critical Incident Analysis**
  8.1 Description
    (a) What did the client say or do at that particular point?
    (b) What did you say or do?
    (c) How did the client respond to your intervention?
    (d) What was happening within you?
  8.2 Analysis
    (a) What was happening within the client?
    (b) What was going on between you and the client?
    (c) Intention and impact of interventions/responses.
    (d) What hunches/hypotheses did you/do you have?
    (e) Review. Any further/alternative perspectives, strategies and interventions.

9. **Listening to Aspects of Covert Communication**
  9.1 What was happening within you? How well can you listen to your own emotional response to a client? You may be aware of your feelings first and thoughts later. Reflection on your emotional experience may help you gain information about what part of the client is likely to be in need of change.
  A simple way of using yourself as a measuring instrument is to ask:
    (a) How does this client make me feel?
    (b) What did the client say and do so that I feel the way I do?
    (c) What does the client want from me and what sort of feeling is she or he trying to arouse in me to get it?
  9.2 What was happening within the client?
  Different kinds of listening to pick up on whatever is live and poignant for the client at a particular moment. The emphasis is on aspects of covert experience, rather than on explicit content.

You can learn to listen for/observe and reflect back when appropriate.

(a) Changes in voice quality – which might indicate an inner focus on something that is being seen or felt differently.

(b) Highly sensory/idiosyncratic words or phrases.

(c) Aspects of content you don't actually understand – perhaps the client doesn't either.

(d) Encoded statements – about other people or situations which may at some level be about the client with reformulations. For example, a client says: 'It upset me to see the little dog was alone'. A reformulation might be: 'Seeing the little dog gave you a sense of desolation and rejection. Something about loneliness worries you'.

Reformulation to focus on the client can be practised almost as a game in supervision.

(e) Indirect or disguised communication. Anything said about something out there may be about you and/or the counselling relationship. Use immediacy.

(f) Non-verbal communication, e.g. silence, gazing into space, posture. Try a hunch about the client's inner experience.

2   BAC *Code of Ethics and Practice for the Supervision of Counsellors*

A   Introduction

A.1   The purpose of this Code of Ethics is to establish standards for Supervisors in their supervision work with Counsellors, and to inform and protect Counsellors seeking supervision.

A.2   Ethical standards comprise such values as integrity, competence, confidentiality and responsibility.

A.3   This document should be seen in relation to the Code of Ethics and Practice for Counsellors. NB: The appropriate

Code to be used by those involved in the supervision of trainees is the Code of Ethics & Practice for Trainers.

A.4 Members of this Association, in assenting to this Code, accept their responsibilities to counsellors and their clients, their agencies, to colleagues, and this Association.

A.5 There are various models of supervision. The Code applies to all supervision arrangements.

The Code of Ethics has three sections:
1 The Nature of Supervision
2 Issues of Responsibility
3 Issues of Competence

The Code of Practice has two sections:
1 The Management of the Supervision Work
2 Confidentiality

The Appendix describes different models of Supervision, and comments on issues that may be relevant to particular models.

B   Code of Ethics

B.1 The Nature of Supervision

1.1 The primary purpose of supervision is to ensure that the counsellor is addressing the needs of the client.

1.2 Supervision is a formal collaborative process. The term 'supervision' encompasses a number of functions concerned with monitoring, developing, and supporting individuals in their counselling role. (This process is sometimes known as 'non-managerial supervision' or 'consultative support'.)

1.3 To this end supervision is concerned with:

(a) the relationship between counsellor and client, to enhance its therapeutic effectiveness.

(b) monitoring and supporting the counsellor in the counselling role.

(c) the relationship between the counsellor and the supervisor, in order to enable the counsellor to develop his/her professional identity through reflection on the work, in the context of this relationship, which will be both critical and supportive.

(d) clarifying the relationship between counsellor, client, supervisor, and (if any) the organisation(s) involved.

(e) ensuring that ethical standards are maintained throughout the counselling work.

1.4   Supervision is therefore not primarily concerned with:
    (a) training
    (b) personal counselling of the counsellor
    (c) line management
        However, the skills associated with these activities are central to competent supervision.
1.5   The supervisory relationship must by its nature be confidential.
1.6   A counsellor should not work without regular supervision.

B.2 Issues of responsibility

2.1   Given that the primary purpose of supervision is to ensure that the counsellor is addressing the needs of the client:
    (a) counsellors are responsible for their work with the client, and for presenting and exploring as honestly as possible that work with the supervisor.
    (b) Supervisors are responsible for helping counsellors reflect critically upon that work.
    It is important that both parties are able to work together effectively. (See C.2.1 to C.2.4.)
2.2   Supervisors are responsible with counsellors for ensuring that they make best use of the supervision time.
2.3   Supervisors and counsellors are both responsible for setting and maintaining clear boundaries between working relationships and friendships or other relationships, and making explicit the boundaries between supervision, consultancy, therapy and training.
2.4   Supervisors and counsellors must distinguish between supervising and counselling the counsellor. They would not normally expect to mix the two. On the rare occasions when the supervisor might engage in counselling with the counsellor, a clear contract must be negotiated, and any counselling done must not be at the expense of supervision time.
2.5   Supervisors are responsible for the observation of the principles embodied in this Code of Ethics & Practice for the Supervision of Counsellors, and the Code of Ethics & Practice for Counsellors.
2.6   Supervisors must recognise the value and dignity of counsellors as people, irrespective of origin, status, sex, sexual orientation, age, belief or contribution to society.
2.7   Supervisors are responsible for encouraging and facilitating the self-development of others, whilst also establishing clear working agreements which indicate the responsibility of

counsellors for their own continued learning and self-monitoring.

2.8 Both are responsible for regularly reviewing the effectiveness of the supervision arrangement, and considering when it is appropriate to change it.

2.9 Supervisors are responsible for ensuring that the satisfaction of their own needs is not dependent upon the supervisory relationship, and they should not exploit this relationship.

2.10 The supervisor and counsellor should both consider their respective legal liabilities to each other, the employing organisation, if any, and the client.

B.3 Issues of Competence

3.1 Supervisors should continually seek ways of increasing their own professional development, including, wherever possible, specific training in the development of supervision skills.

3.2 Supervisors must monitor their supervision work and be prepared to account to their counsellors and colleagues for the work they do.

3.3 Supervisors must monitor the limits of their competence.

3.4 Supervisors are strongly encouraged to make arrangements for their own consultancy and support to help them evaluate their supervision work.

3.5 Supervisors have a responsibility to monitor and maintain their own effectiveness. There may be a need to seek help and/or withdraw from the practice of supervision, whether temporarily or permanently.

3.6 Counsellors should consider carefully the implications of choosing a supervisor who is not a practising counsellor. This applies especially to inexperienced counsellors.

C   Code of Practice

C.1 Introduction

This Code of Practice is intended to give more specific information and guidance regarding the implementation of the principles embodied in the Code of Ethics for the Supervision of Counsellors.

C.2 The Management of the Supervision Work

In order to establish an effective supervision contract, the following points should be considered:

2.1 Supervisors should inform counsellors as appropriate about their own training, philosophy and theoretical approach, qualifications, and the methods they use.

2.2 Supervisors should be explicit regarding practical arrangements for supervision, paying particular regard to the length of contact time, the frequency of contact and the privacy of the venue.

2.3 Fees required should be arranged in advance.

2.4 Supervisors and counsellors should make explicit the expectations and requirements they have of each other, and each party should assess the value of working with the other.

2.5 Before embarking on a supervision contract, supervisors should ascertain what, if any, therapeutic or helping relationships the counsellor has had, or is currently engaged in. This is in order to establish any effect this may have on the counsellor's counselling work.

2.6 If, in the course of supervision, it appears that counselling or therapy would be beneficial to a counsellor, the supervisor should discuss the issue and, if appropriate, make a suitable referral to a third party or agency.

2.7 Supervisors should ensure that counsellors are given regular opportunities to discuss and evaluate their experiences of supervision.

2.8 Supervisors should regularly review how the counsellor engages in self-assessment and self-evaluation of their work.

2.9 Supervisors should ensure that counsellors understand the importance of further training experiences, and encourage the counsellor's professional development in this way.

2.10 Supervisors must ensure that counsellors are made aware of the distinction between counselling, accountability to management, consultancy, support, supervision and training.

2.11 Because there is a distinction between line management and counselling supervision, where a counsellor works in an organisation or agency, the lines of accountability and responsibility need to be clearly defined, between: counsellor/client; supervisor/counsellor; organisation/client; organisation/supervisor; organisation/counsellor; supervisor/client.

2.12 Supervisors who become aware of a conflict between their obligation to a counsellor and their obligation to an employing organisation will make explicit to the counsellor the nature of the loyalties and responsibilities involved.

2.13 Where personal disagreements cannot be resolved by discussion between supervisor and counsellor, the supervisor should consult with a fellow professional and, if appropriate, offer to refer the counsellor to another supervisor.

2.14 In addition to the routine self-monitoring of their work, supervisors are strongly encouraged to arrange for regular evaluation of their work by an appropriately experienced consultant.

2.15 Supervisors should, whenever possible, seek further training experience that is relevant to their supervision work.

2.16 Supervisors should take account of the limitations of their competence, and arrange consultations or referrals when appropriate.

C.3 Confidentiality

3.1 As a general principle, supervisors must maintain confidentiality with regard to information about counsellors or clients, with the exceptions cited in C.3.2, C.3.3 and C.3.4.

3.2 Supervisors must not reveal confidential information concerning counsellors or clients to any other person or through any public medium unless:

(a) it is clearly stated in the supervision contract that this is acceptable to both parties, or

(b) when the supervisor considers it is necessary to prevent serious emotional or physical damage to the client.

When the initial contract is being made, agreement about the people to whom a supervisor may speak must include the people on whom the supervisor relies for support, supervision or consultancy. There must also be clarity at this stage about the boundaries of confidentiality regarding people (other than the counsellor) to whom the supervisor may be accountable.

3.3 Confidentiality does not preclude the disclosure of confidential information relating to counsellors when relevant to the following:

(a) recommendations concerning counsellors for professional purposes.

(b) pursuit of disciplinary action involving counsellors in matters pertaining to ethical standards.

3.4 Information about specific counsellors may only be used for publication in journals or meetings with the counsellor's permission, and with anonymity preserved when the counsellor so specifies.

3.5 Discussion by supervisors of counsellors with professional colleagues should be purposeful and not trivialising.

D   Appendix

D.1 Models of Supervision

1.1   There are different models of supervision. This appendix outlines the particular features of some of these models.

1.2   One-to-one: Supervisor-Counsellor:
This involves a single supervisor providing supervision for one other counsellor, who is usually less experienced than themselves in counselling. This is still the most widely used method of supervision. Its long history means that most of the issues requiring the supervisor's and counsellor's consideration are well understood, and these are included within the Code of Practice above.

1.3   One-to-one: Co-supervision
This involves two participants providing supervision for each other by alternating the roles of supervisor and counsellor. Typically, the time available for a supervision session is divided equally between them.

1.4   Group supervision with identified supervisor(s):
There are a range of ways of providing this form of supervision. At one end of the spectrum the supervisor, acting as the leader, will take responsibility for apportioning the time between the counsellors, and then concentrating on the work of individuals in turn. At the other end of the range, the counsellors will allocate supervision time between themselves, using the supervisor as a technical resource. There are many different ways of working between these two alternatives.

1.5   Peer group supervision:
This takes place when three or more counsellors share the responsibility for providing each others' supervision within a group context. Typically, they will consider themselves to be of broadly equal status, training and/or experience.

1.6   Eclectic methods of supervision:
Some counsellors use combinations of the above models for their supervision.

D.2 Points requiring additional consideration

2.1   Certain models require the consideration of some of the points listed below, that are additional to the contents of the Code of Practice

Types of Supervision (See below D.2):	Points for Consideration 2 3 4 5 6 7 8 9
1.2 One-to-one: Supervisor-Counsellor	X
1.3 One-to-one: Co-supervision	X X X X
1.4 Group supervision with identified supervisors	X X X X X
1.5 Peer group supervision	X X X X – X X X
1.6 Eclectic model	All relevant points.

2   All the points contained elsewhere within the Code of Practice should be considered.

3   Sufficient time must be allocated to each counsellor to ensure adequate supervision of the counselling work.

4   This method is unlikely to be suitable for newly trained or inexperienced counsellors, because of the importance of supervisors being experienced in counselling.

5   Care needs to be taken to develop an atmosphere conducive to sharing, questioning and challenging each others' practice in a constructive way.

6   As well as having a background in counselling work, supervisors should have appropriate groupwork experience in order to facilitate this kind of group.

7   All the participants should have sufficient groupwork experience to be able to engage the group process in ways in which facilitate effective supervision.

8   Explicit consideration should be given to deciding who is responsible for providing the supervision, and how the task of supervision will be carried out.

9   It is desirable that these groups are visited from time to time by a consultant to observe the group process and monitor the quality of the supervision.

British Association for Counselling, 1988. Reproduced with permission.
All BAC Codes of Ethics are subject to change at each year's Annual General Meeting. Details of current Codes of Practice should be confirmed with the British Association for Counselling.

3   Therapist intentions

1 To set limits or make arrangements: To structure, establish goals and objectives of treatment, outline methods to attain goals, correct expectations about treatment, or establish rules or parameters of relationship (e.g., time, length, fees, cancellation policies, homework, content, etc.).

2 To gather information: To find out specific facts about history, client functioning, future plans etc.

3 To give information: To educate, give facts, correct misperceptions or misinformation, give reasons for therapist's behaviour or procedures.

4 To support and build rapport: To provide a warm, supportive, empathic environment; to increase trust and rapport and build relationship, to help client feel accepted, understood, supported, comfortable, reassured, and less anxious: to help establish a person-to-person relationship.

5 To focus: To help client focus, get back on track, change subject, channel or structure the discussion if he/she is unable to begin or if he/she has been diffuse, rambling, or shifting topics.

6 To clarify: To provide or solicit more elaboration, emphasis, or specification when client or therapist has been vague, incomplete, confusing, contradictory, or inaudible.

7 To instill hope: To convey the expectation that change is possible and likely to occur; that the therapist will be able to help the client; to restore morale; to build up the client's confidence to make changes.

8 To promote relief from tension or unhappy feelings: To allow the client a chance to cathart, let go, or talk through feelings and problems.

9 To identify maladaptive cognitions: To point out illogical or irrational thoughts or attitudes (e.g., 'I must be perfect' etc.).

From: C. Hill and K.E. O'Grady (1985) 'List of therapist intentions illustrated in a case study and with therapists of varying theoretical orientations', Journal of Counseling Psychology, 32: 3–22.

10 To identify maladaptive behaviours: To give feedback about the client's inappropriate behaviour and/or its consequences; to do a behavioural analysis; to point out games.

11 To encourage a sense of self-control: To help the client own or gain a sense of mastery or control over his/her own thoughts, feelings, behaviours, or impulses; to help become more appropriately internal rather than inappropriately external in taking responsibility for one's role.

12 To identify, intensify, and/or enable acceptance of feelings: To encourage or provoke the client to become aware of or deepen underlying or hidden feelings or affect or to experience feelings at a deeper level.

13 To stimulate insight: To encourage understanding of the underlying reasons, dynamics, assumptions, or unconscious motivations for cognitions, behaviours, attitudes or feelings. May include an understanding of the client's reactions to others' behaviours.

14 To build more appropriate behaviours or cognitions: To help develop new and more adaptive skills, behaviours, or cognitions to inculcate new ways of dealing with self and others. May be to instill new, more adaptive assumptive models, frameworks, explanations or conceptualisations. May be to give an assessment, or opinion about client functioning that will help client see self in a new way.

15 To reinforce change attempts: To give positive reinforcement of feedback about behavioural, cognitive, or affective attempts at change in order to enhance the probability that the change will be continued or maintained; to encourage risk-taking and new ways of behaving.

16 To overcome obstacles to change: To analyze lack of progress, resistance, or failure to adhere to therapeutic procedures, either past or possibilities of relapse in future.

17 To challenge: To jolt the client out of a present state; to shake up current beliefs or feelings; to test validity; adequacy, reality, or appropriateness of beliefs, thoughts, feelings, or behaviours; to help client question the necessity of maintaining old patterns.

18 To resolve problems in the therapeutic relationship: To deal with issues as they arise in the relationship in order to build or maintain a smooth working alliance; to heal ruptures in the alliance; to deal with dependency issues appropriate to stage in treatment; to uncover and resolve distortions in client's thinking about the relationship which are based on past experiences rather than current reality.

19 To relieve therapist: To protect or defend the therapist, to take care of the therapist's needs; to alleviate anxiety; to try unduly to persuade, argue, or feel good or superior at the expense of the client.

4   Competencies of supervisors

	Needs Development	Expertise

I. Conceptual Skills and Knowledge

A *Generic Skills*
The supervisor is able to demonstrate knowledge and conceptual understanding of the following:

	Needs Development				Expertise
1 the methodology of supervision, including	1	2	3	4	5
(a) facilitative processes (consultation, counseling, education, or training and evaluation).	1	2	3	4	5
(b) basic approaches (e.g., psycho-therapeutic, behavioral, integrative, systems, developmental).	1	2	3	4	5
2 a definition or explanation of supervision	1	2	3	4	5
3 the variety of settings in which counselor supervisors work.	1	2	3	4	5
4 the counselor's roles and functions in particular work settings.	1	2	3	4	5
5 the developmental nature of supervision	1	2	3	4	5
6 appropriate supervisory interventions, including	1	2	3	4	5
(a) role-playing.	1	2	3	4	5
(b) role-reversal.	1	2	3	4	5
(c) live observation and live supervision.	1	2	3	4	5
(d) reviewing audio and videotapes.	1	2	3	4	5
(e) giving direct suggestions and advice.	1	2	3	4	5
(f) leading groups of 2 or more supervisees.	1	2	3	4	5

From: L.D. Borders and G.R. Leddick (1987) *Handbook of Counseling Supervision*. Alexandria, VA: Association for Counselor Education and Supervision

(g)	providing didactic experiences.	1	2	3	4	5
(h)	microtraining.	1	2	3	4	5
(i)	IPR.	1	2	3	4	5
(j)	other _____	1	2	3	4	5
7	credentialing standards for counselors.	1	2	3	4	5
8	counselor ethical practices.	1	2	3	4	5
9	various counseling theories.	1	2	3	4	5
10	his/her own personal theory of counseling.	1	2	3	4	5
11	his/her assumptions about human behavior.	1	2	3	4	5
12	models of supervision.	1	2	3	4	5
13	the meaning of accountability and the supervisor's responsibility in promoting this condition.	1	2	3	4	5
14	human growth and development.	1	2	3	4	5
15	motivation and needs theory.	1	2	3	4	5
16	learning theory.	1	2	3	4	5
17	resources and information to assist in addressing program goals and client needs.	1	2	3	4	5

B **Supervision of Practicing Counselors**
The supervisor is able to demonstrate knowledge and conceptual understanding of the following:

18	legal considerations affecting counselor practice.	1	2	3	4	5
19	various intervention activities and strategies that would complement the counseling program goals.	1	2	3	4	5

C **Supervision of Counselors-in-Training**
(covered in Generic Skills above)

D **Program Management/Supervision**
The supervisor is able to demonstrate knowledge and conceptual understanding of the following:

20	his/her basic management theory.	1	2	3	4	5
21	various program development models.	1	2	3	4	5
22	decision-making theory.	1	2	3	4	5
23	organization development theory.	1	2	3	4	5
24	conflict resolution techniques.	1	2	3	4	5
25	leadership styles.	1	2	3	4	5
26	computerized information systems.	1	2	3	4	5
27	time-management techniques.	1	2	3	4	5

II   Direct Intervention Skills

A   *Generic Skills*
The supervisor is able to demonstrate
intervention techniques in the following
ways:

1   provide structure for supervision sessions,   1   2   3   4   5
    including
    (a) stating the purpose of supervision.   1   2   3   4   5
    (b) clarifying the goals and direction of   1   2   3   4   5
         supervision.
    (c) clarifying his/her own role in   1   2   3   4   5
         supervision.
    (d) explaining the procedures to be   1   2   3   4   5
         followed in supervision.
2   identify the learning needs of the   1   2   3   4   5
    supervisee.
3   determine the extent to which the   1   2   3   4   5
    supervisee has developed and applied
    his/her own personal theory of counseling.
4   provide specific feedback about   1   2   3   4   5
    supervisee's
    (a) conceptualization of client concerns.   1   2   3   4   5
    (b) process of counseling.   1   2   3   4   5
    (c) personalization of counseling.   1   2   3   4   5
    (d) performance of other related duties.   1   2   3   4   5
5   implement a variety of supervisory   1   2   3   4   5
    interventions (see Conceptual Skills &
    Knowledge).
6   negotiate mutual decisions regarding the   1   2   3   4   5
    needed direction of learning experiences
    for the supervisee.
7   use media aids for assisting with   1   2   3   4   5
    supervision.
8   develop evaluation procedures and   1   2   3   4   5
    instruments to determine program and
    supervisee goal attainment.
9   monitor the use of tests and test   1   2   3   4   5
    interpretations.
10 assist with the referral process,   1   2   3   4   5
    when appropriate.
11 facilitate and monitor research to determine   1   2   3   4   5
    the effectiveness of programs, services, and
    techniques.

B *Program Management/Supervision*
The supervisor is able to demonstrate
intervention techniques in the following
ways:

12	develop role descriptions for all staff positions.	1	2	3	4	5
13	conduct a needs assessment.	1	2	3	4	5
14	write goals and objectives.	1	2	3	4	5
15	monitor the progress of program activities.	1	2	3	4	5
16	monitor the progress of staff's responsibilities.	1	2	3	4	5
17	utilize decision-making techniques.	1	2	3	4	5
18	apply problem-solving techniques.	1	2	3	4	5
19	conduct and coordinate staff development training.	1	2	3	4	5
20	implement management information systems.	1	2	3	4	5
21	employ group management strategies.	1	2	3	4	5
22	schedule tasks and develop time lines according to the needs of supervisees and the program.	1	2	3	4	5
23	maintain appropriate forms and records to assist with supervisory duties.	1	2	3	4	5
24	monitor supervisee report-writing and record-keeping skills.	1	2	3	4	5
25	diagnose organizational problems.	1	2	3	4	5
26	employ systematic observation techniques.	1	2	3	4	5
27	plan and administer a budget.	1	2	3	4	5
28	conduct follow-up studies and applied research.	1	2	3	4	5
29	establish consistent and quality hiring and affirmative action practices.	1	2	3	4	5
30	delegate responsibility.	1	2	3	4	5

III Human Skills

A *Generic Skills*
The supervisor is able to apply the
following interaction skills in a supervisory
capacity:

1	deal with the supervisee from the perspective of	1	2	3	4	5
	(a) teacher.	1	2	3	4	5
	(b) counselor.	1	2	3	4	5

(c) consultant.	1	2	3	4	5
(d) evaluator.	1	2	3	4	5

2 describe his/her own pattern of dealing with interpersonal relationships. 1 2 3 4 5

3 integrate knowledge of supervision with own style of inter-personal relations. 1 2 3 4 5

4 create facilitative conditions (empathy, concreteness, respect, congruence, genuineness, and immediacy). 1 2 3 4 5

5 establish a mutually trusting relationship with the supervisee. 1 2 3 4 5

6 establish a therapeutic relationship when appropriate. 1 2 3 4 5

7 identify supervisee's professional and personal strengths, as well as weaknesses. 1 2 3 4 5

8 clarify supervisee's personal needs (behavior mannerisms, personal crises, appearance, etc.), as well as professional needs that affect counseling. 1 2 3 4 5

9 elicit supervisee feelings during counseling or consultation sessions. 1 2 3 4 5

10 elicit supervisee perceptions of counseling dynamics. 1 2 3 4 5

11 use confrontation skills when identifying supervisee's inconsistencies. 1 2 3 4 5

12 elicit new alternatives from supervisee for identifying solutions, techniques, responses, etc. 1 2 3 4 5

13 demonstrate skill in the application of counseling techniques (both individual and group) that are appropriate for the work setting. 1 2 3 4 5

14 assist the supervisee in structuring his/her own self-supervision. 1 2 3 4 5

15 conduct self-evaluation as a means of modeling appropriate professional growth. 1 2 3 4 5

16 identify own strengths and weaknesses as a supervisor. 1 2 3 4 5

17 model appropriate behaviors expected of supervisees. 1 2 3 4 5

18 demonstrate and enforce ethical/professional standards. 1 2 3 4 5

B   *Traits and Qualities*
    The supervisor possesses the following
    traits or qualities:

1   demonstrates a commitment to the role   1 2 3 4 5
    of supervisor.

2   is comfortable with the authority inherent 1 2 3 4 5
    in the role of supervisor.

3   has a sense of humor.   1 2 3 4 5

4   is encouraging, optimistic, and   1 2 3 4 5
    motivational.

5   expects supervisees to own the   1 2 3 4 5
    consequences of their actions.

6   is sensitive to individual differences.   1 2 3 4 5

7   is sensitive to supervisee's needs.   1 2 3 4 5

8   is committed to updating his/her own   1 2 3 4 5
    counseling and supervisory skills.

9   recognizes that the ultimate goal of   1 2 3 4 5
    supervision is helping the client of the
    supervisee.

10 maintains open communication between   1 2 3 4 5
    supervisees and the supervisor.

11 monitors the 'energy level' of supervisees 1 2 3 4 5
    to identify possible signs of counselor
    burnout in advance of possible crises.

12 recognizes own limits through eliciting   1 2 3 4 5
    self-evaluation and
    feedback from others.

13 enjoys and appreciates the role of   1 2 3 4 5
    supervisor.

This list of supervision competencies was adopted by the ACES Supervision Interest
Network (C.E. VanZandt, Chair), at the AACD Convention, New York, April 2, 1985

5   BAC *Recognition of Supervisors Details*

Criteria for the Recognition of Supervisors

The successful applicant will be one who:

1   Is either a BAC Accredited counsellor or has training and experience appropriate to that standard.

2   Has had training in supervision, either by attending an appropriate course or by having had training from an experienced supervisor.

3   Has had at least 100 hours of supervision experience over a period of not less than two years with a minimum of four individual supervisees and one group.

4   Has a philosophy of supervision which integrates training, experience and practice. Evidence of theoretical knowledge should be demonstrated.

5   Has regular access to a supervisory consultant or group for their supervisory work.

6   Demonstrates practice which adheres to the BAC Code of Ethics & Practice for the Supervision of Counsellors and undertakes to continue working under this Code.

7   Demonstrates the ability to work with the triangular relationship specific to counselling supervision.

8   Is a current individual member of BAC.

Applicants are required to give evidence of the above in the form of a written application, a presentation of a piece of their own supervision of a counsellor; and to take part in a

Recognition Day which will include giving and receiving live supervision, and discussion of both written and live material with assessors.

Assessors will be looking for congruence between all parts of the application as well as checking that the above criteria are being met.

Recognition Procedure

Applicants will be required to provide the following material:

1 A completed application form.
2 A presentation of a piece of their supervision preferably of an individual counsellor, including reactions of the supervisee. This can be in the form of either:
   (a) A written verbatim of a supervision session, with process commentary.
   (b) A tape (not exceeding 45 minutes in length), with a written process commentary.
   (c) A video (not exceeding 45 minutes in length), with a written process commentary.
3 A description of their aims and methods, including an account of their philosophical and psychological understanding of supervision, normally expected to be 1500–2000 words.

The Recognition Process

1 The application, together with the comments of the consultant/ supervisor will be shared with the assessors. All the assessors are supervisors recognised by BAC.
2 The application will initially be sent to an assessor and a preliminary assessment made of the material presented. Providing that, in the opinion of the assessor, the material in the application initially appears to meet the criteria, the applicant will be invited to attend an assessment day. An agreement from the preliminary assessor, does NOT guarantee that the applicant will receive recognition. Applicants whose material does not meet the criteria will be informed of the discrepancies and given guidance about what is required additionally.
3 On the Recognition Day, applicants will take part in a live assessment of their supervision where they will normally, though not always, be supervising each other. It is important to be aware that supervisees will all be experienced counsellors.

Applicants should bring a piece of current counselling work on which they will be supervised by one of the peer group being assessed. Applicants will then be interviewed by their assessor when they will have an opportunity to discuss both their live presentation and their submitted material.

4   The live work is assessed on both the openness to receiving supervision as well as giving it. However, the live work is not rated more highly than the written and recorded material. The assessors will be looking for congruence between the written material and the live presentation.

5   The recognition is for ten years after which time you will be invited to participate in whatever renewal procedure is in operation.

6   Applicants may supervise experienced candidates who may not be the same orientation as themselves.

British Association for Counselling, 1993.
Reproduced with permission.

References

Austin, K.M., Moline, M.E. and Williams, G.T. (1990) *Confronting Malpractice: Legal and Ethical Dilemmas in Psychotherapy.* Newbury Park, CA: Sage.

BAC (1990) *The Recognition of Counsellor Training Courses.* Rugby: British Association for Counselling.

Back, K.W. (1973) *Beyond Words: The Story of Sensitivity Training and the Encounter Movement.* Baltimore, MA: Penguin.

Barkham, M. (1990) 'Research in individual therapy', in W. Dryden (ed.), *Individual Therapy: A Handbook.* Milton Keynes: Open University Press.

Bayne, R. (1993) 'Psychological type, conversations and counselling', in R. Bayne and P. Nicolson (eds), *Counselling and Psychology for Health Professionals.* London: Chapman and Hall.

Bernard, J.M. and Goodyear, R.K. (1992) *Fundamentals of Clinical Supervision.* Boston, MA: Allyn and Bacon.

Borders, L.D. and Leddick, G.R. (1987) *Handbook of Counseling Supervision.* Alexandria, VA: Association for Counselor Education and Supervision.

Bordin, E.S. (1983) 'A working alliance based model of supervision', *The Counseling Psychologist,* 11 (1): 35–42.

BPS (1993) *Regulations for the Diploma in Counselling Psychology.* Leicester: British Psychological Society.

Bradley, L.J. (1989) *Counselor Supervision* (2nd edn). Muncie, IN: Accelerated Development.

Brammer, L.M. and Wassmer, A.C. (1977) 'Supervision in counseling and psychotherapy', in D.J. Kurpius, R.D. Baker and I.D. Thomas (eds), *Supervision of Applied Training.* Westport, CT: Greenwood.

Budman, S.H., Hoyt, M.F. and Friedman, S. (eds) (1992) *The First Session in Brief Therapy.* New York: Guilford.

Burns, D.D. (1980) *Feeling Good: The New Mood Therapy.* New York: Signet.

Casement, P. (1985) *On Learning from the Patient.* London: Tavistock.

Cohen, L. (1980) 'The new supervisee views supervision', in A.K. Hess (ed.), *Psychotherapy Supervision.* New York: Wiley.

Conn, J.D. (1993) 'Delicate liaisons: the impact of gender differences on the supervisory relationship within social services', *Journal of Social Work Practice,* 7 (1): 41–53.

Covner, B.J. (1944) 'Studies in phonographic recordings of verbal material: III. The completeness and accuracy of counseling interview reports', *Journal of General Psychology,* 30: 181–203.

Davenport, D.S. (1992) 'Ethical and legal problems with client-centred supervision', *Counselor Education and Supervision,* 31 (4): 227–31.

Davis, J. (1989) 'Issues in the evaluation of counsellors by supervisors', *Counselling,* 69: 31–7.

De Shazer, S. (1985) *Keys to Solution in Brief Therapy.* New York: Norton.

Doehrman, M.J.G. (1976) 'Parallel processes in supervision and psychotherapy', *Bulletin of the Menninger Clinic,* 40: part 1.

Dryden, W. (1982) Vivid RET. Ruislip: Institute for RET.

Dryden, W. (1991a) Dryden on Counselling. Vol. 3: Training and Supervision. London: Whurr.

Dryden, W. (ed.) (1991b) The Essential Arnold Lazarus. London: Whurr.

Dryden, W. (1991c) A Dialogue with Arnold Lazarus: 'It Depends'. Buckingham: Open University Press.

Dryden, W. (1992) The Dryden Interviews: Dialogues on the Psychotherapeutic Process. London: Whurr.

Dryden, W. and Feltham, C. (1992) Brief Counselling: A Practical Guide for Beginning Practitioners. Buckingham: Open University Press.

Dryden, W. and Feltham, C. (1994a) Developing Counsellor Training. London: Sage.

Dryden, W. and Feltham, C. (1994b) Developing the Practice of Counselling. London: Sage.

Dryden, W. and Spurling, L. (eds) (1989) On Becoming a Psychotherapist. London: Routledge.

Dryden, W. and Varma, V. (eds) (1994) Stresses of Counselling in Action. London: Sage.

Egan, G. (1990) The Skilled Helper (4th edn). Pacific Grove, CA: Brooks/Cole.

Feltham, C. and Dryden, W. (1993) Dictionary of Counselling. London: Whurr.

Fisher, B.L. (1989) 'Differences between supervision of beginning and advanced therapists: Hogan's hypothesis empirically revisited', The Clinical Supervisor, 7: 57–74.

Frances, A., Sweeney, J. and Clarkin, J. (1985) 'Do psychotherapies have specific effects?', American Journal of Psychotherapy, 39 (2): 159–74.

Frank, J.D. (1973) Persuasion and Healing. Baltimore, MA: The Johns Hopkins University Press.

Friedlander, M.L., Siegel, S. and Brenock, K. (1989) 'Parallel processes in counseling and supervision: a case study', Journal of Counseling Psychology, 36: 149–57.

Goldberg, C. (1992) The Seasoned Psychotherapist. New York: Norton.

Goldberg, D.A. (1985) 'Process notes, audio and video tapes: modes of presentation in psychotherapy training', The Clinical Supervisor, 3: 3–13.

Goodyear, R.K. and Robyak, J.E. (1982) Psychological Reports, 51, 978.

Guy, J.D. (1987) The Personal Life of the Psychotherapist. New York: Wiley.

Hallam, R. (1992) Counselling for Anxiety Problems. London: Sage.

Hart, G.M. (1982) The Process of Clinical Supervision. Baltimore, MA: University Park Press.

Hawkins, P. and Shohet, R. (1989) Supervision in the Helping Professions. Milton Keynes: Open University Press.

Heron, J. (1990) Helping the Client. London: Sage.

Hess, A.K. (ed.) (1980) Psychotherapy Supervision. New York: Wiley.

Hess, A.K. (1986) 'Growth in supervision: stages of supervisee and supervisor development', in F.W. Kaslow (ed.), Supervision and Training: Models, Dilemmas and Challenges. New York: Haworth.

Hill, C.E. and O'Grady, K.E. (1985) 'List of therapist intentions illustrated in a case study and with therapists of varying theoretical orientations', Journal of Counseling Psychology, 32: 3–22.

Hill, C.E., Helms, J.E., Spiegel, S.B. and Tichenor, V. (1988) 'Development of a system for categorizing client reactions to therapist interventions', Journal of Counseling Psychology, 35 (1): 27–36.

Holloway, E.L. (1992) 'Supervision: a way of teaching and learning', in S.D. Brown and R.W. Lent (eds), Handbook of Counseling Psychology (2nd edn). New York: Wiley.

Hope, D. (1989) 'The evaluation of counselling services and counsellors in the United States', Counselling, 69: 19–25.

Horton, I. (1993) 'Supervision', in R. Bayne and P. Nicolson (eds), Counselling and Psychology for Health Professionals. London: Chapman and Hall.

Houston, G. (1990) Supervision and Counselling. London: Rochester Foundation.

Howard, A. (1992) 'What, and why are we accrediting?', Counselling, 3 (3): 171–3.

Howe, D. (1989) The Consumers' View of Family Therapy. Aldershot: Gower.

Inskipp, F. and Proctor, B. (1989) Being Supervised: Audio-tape 1, Principles of Counselling. St. Leonards-on-Sea: Alexia Publications.

Ivey, A.E., Ivey, M.B. and Simek-Downing, L. (1987) Counseling and Psychotherapy: Integrating Skills, Theory and Practice (2nd edn). Englewood Cliffs, NJ: Prentice-Hall.

Kadushin, A. (1968) 'Games people play in supervision', Social Work, 13: 23–32.

Kagan, N. (1980) 'Influencing human interaction – eighteen years with IPR', in A.K. Hess (ed.), Psychotherapy Supervision: Theory, Research and Practice. New York: Wiley.

Kopp, S. (1977) Back to One. Palo Alto, CA: Science and Behavior.

Lambert, M.J., Shapiro, D.A. and Bergin, A.E. (1986) 'The effectiveness of psychotherapy', in S.L. Garfield and A.E. Bergin (eds), Handbook of Psychotherapy and Behavior Change (3rd edn). New York: Wiley.

Lazarus, A.A. (1989) The Practice of Multimodal Therapy. Baltimore, MA: The Johns Hopkins University Press.

Loganbill, C., Hardy, E. and Delworth, U. (1982) 'Supervision: a conceptual model', The Counseling Psychologist, 10 (1): 3–42.

Lukas, S. (1993) Where to Start and What to Say: An Assessment Handbook. New York: Norton.

Masson, J.M. (1988) Against Therapy. New York: Atheneum.

Mattinson, J. (1975) The Reflection Process in Casework Supervision. London: Institute of Marital Studies.

Mearns, D. (1990) 'The counsellor's experience of success', in D. Mearns and W. Dryden (eds), Experience of Counselling in Action. London: Sage.

Mearns, D. (1991) 'On being a supervisor', in W. Dryden and B. Thorne (eds), Training and Supervision for Counselling in Action. London: Sage.

Moore, J. (1991) 'On being a supervisee', in W. Dryden and B. Thorne (eds), Training and Supervision for Counselling in Action. London: Sage.

Muslin, H.L., Thurnblad, R.J. and Meschel, G. (1981) 'The fate of the clinical interview: an observational study', American Journal of Psychiatry, 138 (6): 825–33.

Norcross, J.C. and Guy, J.D. (1989) 'Ten therapists: the process of becoming and being', in W. Dryden and L. Spurling (eds), On Becoming a Psychotherapist. London: Routledge.

Park, J. (1992) Shrinks: The Analysts Analyzed. London: Bloomsbury.

Proctor, B. (1987) 'Supervision: a co-operative exercise in accountability', in M. Marken and M. Payne (eds), Enabling and Ensuring: Supervision in Practice. Leicester: National Youth Bureau.

Progoff, I. (1975) At a Journal Workshop. New York: Dialogue House.

Regan, A.M. and Hill, C.E. (1992) 'Investigation of what clients and counsellors do not say in brief therapy', *Journal of Counseling Psychology*, 39 (2): 168–74.

Reising, G.N. and Daniels, M.H. (1983) 'A study of Hogan's model of counselor development and supervision', *Journal of Counseling Psychology*, 30: 235–44.

Rioch, M.J. (1980) 'The dilemmas of supervision in dynamic psychotherapy', in A.K. Hess (ed.), *Psychotherapy Supervision: Theory, Research and Practice*. New York: Wiley.

Robertiello, R.C. and Schoenewolf, G.S. (1987) *101 Common Therapeutic Blunders*. New York: Aronson.

Ronnestad, M.H. and Skovholt, T.M. (1993) 'Supervision of beginning and advanced graduate students of counseling and psychotherapy', *Journal of Counseling and Development*, 71: 396–405.

Rusk, T. (1991) *Instead of Therapy*. Carson, CA: Hay House.

Russell, J. (1993) *Out of Bounds: Sexual Exploitation in Counselling and Therapy*. London: Sage.

Rutter, P. (1990) *Sex in the Forbidden Zone*. London: Mandala.

Ryle, G. (1949) *The Concept of Mind*. London: Hutchinson.

Samuels, A. (1989) *The Plural Psyche*. London: Routledge.

Searles, H.F. (1955) 'The informational value of the supervisor's emotional experience', in *Collected Papers on Schizophrenia and Related Subjects*. London: Hogarth Press.

Skovholt, T.M. and Ronnestad, M.H. (1992a) *The Evolving Professional Self: Stages and Themes in Therapist and Counselor Development*. New York: Wiley.

Skovholt, T.M. and Ronnestad, M.H. (1992b) 'Themes in therapist and counselor development', *Journal of Counseling and Development*, 70: 505–15.

Slovenko, R. (1980) 'Legal issues in psychotherapy supervision', in A.K. Hess (ed.), *Psychotherapy Supervision: Theory, Research and Practice*. New York: Wiley.

Smith, D.L. (1991) *Hidden Conversations: An Introduction to Communicative Psychoanalysis*. London: Routledge.

Smith. M.L., Glass, G.C. and Miller, T.I. (1980) *The Benefits of Psychotherapy*. Baltimore, MA: The Johns Hopkins University Press.

Stoltenberg, C.D. and Delworth, U. (1987) *Supervising Counselors and Therapists*. San Francisco: Jossey-Bass.

Striano, J. (1988) *Can Psychotherapists Harm You?* Santa Barbara, CA: Professional Press.

Strozier, A.L., Kivlighan, D.M. and Thoreson, R.W. (1993) 'Supervisor intentions, supervisee reactions, and helpfulness: a case study of the process of supervision', *Professional Psychology: Research and Practice*, 24, (1): 13–19.

Strupp, H.H., Hadley, S.W. and Gomes-Schwartz, B. (1977) *Psychotherapy For Better or Worse*. New York: Aronson.

Thorne, B. (1987) 'Beyond the core conditions', in W. Dryden (ed.), *Key Cases in Psychotherapy*. London: Croom Helm.

Vandecreek, L. and Harrar, W. (1988) 'The legal liability of supervisors', *The Psychotherapy Bulletin*, 23 (3): 13–16.

Varah, C. (ed.) (1985) *The Samaritans: Befriending the Suicidal*. London: Constable.

Wampold, B.E. and Poulin, K.L. (1992) 'Counseling research methods: art and artifact', in S.D. Brown and R.W. Lent (eds), *Handbook of Counseling Psychology* (2nd edn). New York: Wiley.

Wessler, R.L. and Ellis, A. (1980) 'Supervision in rational-emotive therapy', in A.K. Hess (ed.) *Psychotherapy Supervision: Theory, Research and Practice*. New York: Wiley.

Worthington, E.L. (1987) 'Changes in supervision as counselors and supervisors gain experience: a review', *Professional Psychology: Research and Practice*, 18: 189–208.

Index